The SCIENTIFIC AMERICAN
BRAVE NEW
BRAIN

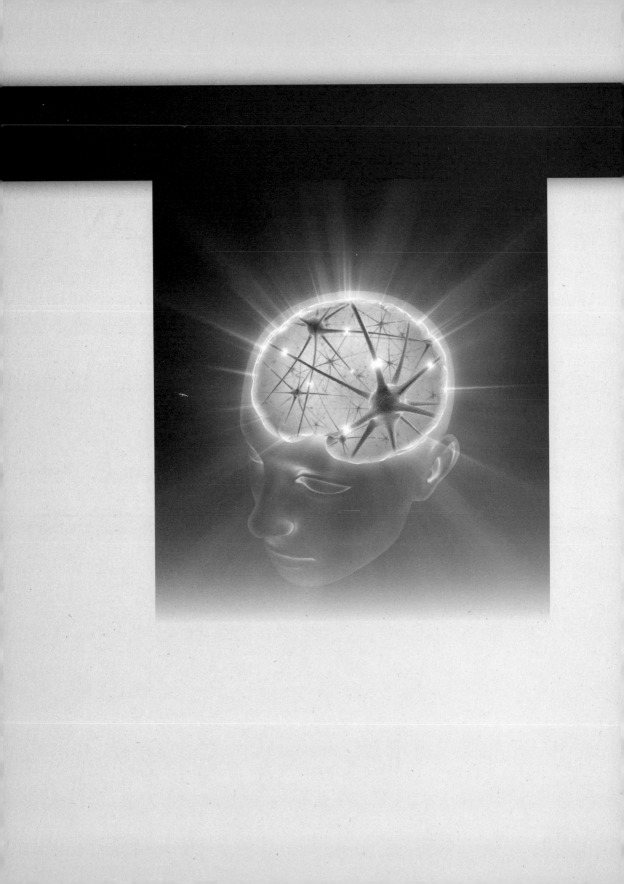

The SCIENTIFIC AMERICAN
BRAVE NEW
BRAIN

Judith Horstman

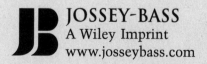

JOSSEY-BASS
A Wiley Imprint
www.josseybass.com

Published by Jossey-Bass
A Wiley Imprint
989 Market Street, San Francisco, CA 94103-1741—www.josseybass.com

The contents of this work are intended to further general scientific research, understanding, and discussion only and are not intended and should not be relied upon as recommending or promoting a specific method, diagnosis, or treatment by physicians for any particular patient. The publisher and the author make no representations or warranties with respect to the accuracy or completeness of the contents of this work and specifically disclaim all warranties, including without limitation any implied warranties of fitness for a particular purpose. In view of ongoing research, equipment modifications, changes in governmental regulations, and the constant flow of information relating to the use of medicines, equipment, and devices, the reader is urged to review and evaluate the information provided in the package insert or instructions for each medicine, equipment, or device for, among other things, any changes in the instructions or indication of usage and for added warnings and precautions. Readers should consult with a specialist where appropriate. The fact that an organization or Web site is referred to in this work as a citation and/or a potential source of further information does not mean that the author or the publisher endorses the information the organization or Web site may provide or recommendations it may make. Further, readers should be aware that Internet Web sites listed in this work may have changed or disappeared between when this work was written and when it is read. No warranty may be created or extended by any promotional statements for this work. Neither the publisher nor the author shall be liable for any damages arising herefrom.

Jossey-Bass books and products are available through most bookstores. To contact Jossey-Bass directly call our Customer Care Department within the U.S. at 800-956-7739, outside the U.S. at 317-572-3986, or fax 317-572-4002.

Jossey-Bass also publishes its books in a variety of electronic formats. Some content that appears in print may not be available in electronic books.

Library of Congress Cataloging-in-Publication Data

Horstman, Judith.
 The Scientific American brave new brain / Judith Horstman. – 1st ed.
  p. cm.
 Includes bibliographical references and index.
 ISBN 978-0-470-37624-9 (cloth)
 1. Brain. 2. Brain–Metabolism. 3. Brain–Physiology. 4. Neurophysiology.
 I. Scientific American. II. Title.
 QP376.H755 2010
 612.8'2–dc22

                 2009048405

Printed in the United States of America
FIRST EDITION
HB Printing   10 9 8 7 6 5 4 3 2 1

CONTENTS

Acknowledgments   xi
Preface   xiii

Introduction   1

1   **Your Changeable Brain:** Neurogenesis, Neuroplasticity,
     and Epigenetics   7
     The Birth of Brain Cells: Neurogenesis   10
     Changes in Your Brain: Neuroplasticity   11
     Changes in Your Genes: Epigenetics   13
     Keeping Your New Brain Cells   14
     No Pain, No Gain   16
     Brain Training Programs: Help or Hype?   17
     What's Next? And What About My Brain?   19

2   **Boosting Your Brain Power**   21
     The Brave New Pharmacy   22
     Juicing the Brain: The "Smart Drugs"   24
     The Caveats: Are These Really "Smart Pills"—and Are
     They Safe?   26
     Six Drug-Free Ways to Boost Your Brain   29
     Boosting Your Brain with Meditation   31
     Meditation Means Changing Your Brain   33
     What's Next? And What About My Brain?   35

3   **Manipulating Your Memory**   37
Memories Are Made of This—We Hope   38
How Memory Works—the Short Version   39
Alzheimer's Disease: The Memory Epidemic   41
What We Know Now About Dementia   43
Marijuana to Ward Off Alzheimer's? Wow.
Like, Cool.   44
Making Memories Stick Around   45
Erasing Bad Memories: A Morning-After Pill
for the Brain   48
The Toll of Mental Illness—and Anxiety   50
What's Next? And What About My Brain?   52

4   **Digital You:** What the Digital Explosion Is Doing
to Your iBrain   55
Are You Born Digital—or a Digital Immigrant?   56
The Brains of Digital Natives   57
The Bad, the Good, and the Unknown Effects of
Technology   59
The Future Is Closer Than You Think   61
Uses of the Digital You   63
What About My Body? Balancing the iBrain and Your
Sensory Self   64
Beyond Digital: The Serious Need for Play   66
What's Next? And What About My Brain?   67

5   **Looking Inside Your Brain:** The Magic of
Neuroimaging   71
Smile, Say Cheese? Not Exactly: How an MRI Works   74
Picture This: Psychopath, Pedophile, Autistic Toddler   76
Scanning the Other Half of Your Brain: Why White
Matter Matters   77
The Limits of Brain Scans   79
The Five Flaws of Brain Scans   80
What's Next? And What About My Brain?   83

6   Rewiring the Brain Electric   87
The Electrical Revolution: A History of Hot-Wiring
Your Head   88
The Current Brain Research: Magnets to
Implants   90
Discovering Depression's Sweet Spot   95
Could Implants Help Alzheimer's Patients?   96
What's Next? And What About My Brain?   97

7   Your Bionic Brain: The Merging of Brain
with Machines   **101**
Spare Parts   102
Bionic Brain Research Today   104
The Britannica in Your Brain—and More   106
Artificial Retinas: Giving Sight to the Blind   107
An Artificial Hippocampus?   108
Putting Thoughts into Action   110
How and Why Your Brain Is Better Than a
Computer—for Now   112
What's Next? And What About My Brain?   114

8   The Possible Dreams: Stem Cells, Gene Therapy, and
Nanotechnology   **117**
The Future of Stem Cells   120
Retinal Stem Cells from Adults Show Promise   122
The Promise of Gene Therapy   123
Nanomedicine   125
What's Next? And What About My Brain?   127

9   Neuroethics: Facing the Dark Side   **129**
Stem Cells: Still Fighting After All These Years   132
Liar, Liar: Can Brain Scans Reveal the Truth?   133
Responsibility: My Sick Brain Made Me Do It (The Devil
Made Me Do It?)   134
Privacy, Bias, and Self-Incrimination   136

Psychotreatment: Should We Force Psychopharmacological
Therapies?   137
Mental Doping on the Rise: They Jail Athletes,
Don't They?   137
Issues Yet to Come: A Future of Busy Lawyers   138

10   The Past Is Prologue: To the Future   141

Sources   143
Illustration Credits   153
Glossary   155
About the Author   161
Index   163

To the future, and to all of our children
and grandchildren who will make it so,
especially (and always) Alcina, Ariadne,
Isabela, Blue, Raj, and Lulu

ACKNOWLEDGMENTS

I must first thank the writers and editors of *Scientific American* and *Scientific American Mind* for the excellent articles on which so much of this book is based; they are acknowledged in detail in the Sources. I am most grateful to the renowned neuroscientists and experts who graciously gave of their time to help me sort out what might be in the quite near future, and who have contributed much to neuroscience, especially R. Douglas Fields, Joseph LeDoux, Richard Davidson, Philip Kennedy, and Hank Greely, an expert on the legal, ethical, and social issues surrounding this brave new world of neuroscience.

The captivating concept for this book came from the creative and hard-working team at Jossey-Bass, who are much appreciated. For the second time, I want to give heartfelt thanks to executive editor (and my editor) Alan Rinzler and senior editorial assistant Nana Twumasi, who have contributed so much to the shaping and creation of this book; Carol Hartland, production genius; Bev Miller, much more than a copyeditor; ace freelance researcher Brianna Smith; Paula Goldstein, who designed the book's interior; and all the marketing people who put my book in your hands: Jennifer Wenzel, Erin Beam, P. J. Campbell, Karen Warner. At *Scientific American,* Diane McGarvey and Lisa Pallatroni were responsible for finding and approving years of archived material. Thank you.

My family, good friends, and fellow writers have once again listened to me agonize endlessly and rant on about the difficulties of writing about the brain. Many thanks to you all, in particular to first readers Kelly A. Dakin (who corrected many of my errors and added valuable content), Ann Crew, Ferris Buck Kelley, Frank Urbanowski, and literary agent Andrea Hurst (for sending this book my way) and the wonderfully productive and generous writing community of Sacramento.

PREFACE

Yesterday's science fiction is today's science.

Yes, that's a cliché you've been hearing for decades. That's because it's true.

In fact, many of today's discoveries in neuroscience and the accompanying technology have surpassed some science fiction. There have been massive changes in our basic understandings of neuroscience and our tools, and yet we are just beginning to grasp the intricate workings of the human brain—your brain.

Scientific American has been looking to the future for more than a century. For example, it projected and predicted the future of brain research in *Scientific American* special editions in 1999 (*Your Bionic Future*) and again in 2003 (*Better Brains*). And in just the past two years, neuroscientists doing cutting-edge research have been written about in or have written for *Scientific American* and *Scientific American Mind*.

This book is based on many of those articles. We trolled recent years for issues and articles key to what's happening today in brain science, particularly how today's world and the many advances in research and technology are changing our brains every day, and what we can expect in the coming decades. Among the contributors whose work is represented here are outstanding scientist writers at the forefront of brain research.

We've added new research as well—some so new that it was not yet in press when this book was being written. And as you are holding this book in your hands, research is leading to even more new findings. The next wave of knowledge and technology is already forming somewhere out there and is rushing toward us at ever-increasing and inexorable speed. Brave new brain indeed!

About That Title

The resonance with Aldous Huxley's dystopic novel *Brave New World* is intended. There's plenty to be wary about in the new brain science, especially in its application to thought; emotions; predictability of certain actions; invasion of privacy; and the ethical, legal, and civil rights issues it raises.

But it's also a nod to the optimism of Shakespeare whose island-raised and isolated character Miranda, in *The Tempest,* exclaims about the possibilities and wonders of an expanded life when she sees other humans for the first time:

> O wonder!
> How many goodly creatures are there here!
> How beauteous mankind is!
> O brave new world,
> That has such people in't!
>
> *The Tempest* (V.i.198–201)

The SCIENTIFIC AMERICAN
BRAVE NEW
BRAIN

INTRODUCTION

We know more about the brain today than ever before, and a perfect storm of events is supporting even more and better brain knowledge—and better brains.

There is a tremendous surge of research on the brain and tremendous pressure to learn more, and learn it faster, from an aging generation with the will and the means to force these advances: boomers. The first of the boomers, the largest ever demographic group and (even with the recession) the best off financially, are hitting old age, and a group that never took no for an answer is not going gently into that good night; instead, it is kicking, screaming, and raging for a better aging brain.

Billions are being expended on brain research, especially in areas related to dementia, memory loss, and other conditions of aging. The National Institutes of Health (NIH) alone spent $5.2 billion, nearly 20 percent of its total budget, on brain-related projects in 2008. With this expanded funding, researchers are making sweeping inroads in both understanding and manipulating the brain. We've learned more about the brain in the past fifty years than the preceding fifty thousand, and the cooperation among the sciences over the next two decades may even surpass that record. Brain research has moved beyond psychology, psychiatry, and neurology, and married the so-called wet and hard sciences: biology, biochemistry, and chemistry now cohabit with physics, engineering, electronics, computer science, material sciences, statistical analysis, and even information technologies, with advances

1

in technology contributing ever-better, smaller, faster, and smarter devices and techniques.

Scientists and futurists are predicting what will have changed by midcentury:

- Computer chips or mini-microprocessors in the brain will expand memory; control symptoms of brain disease, from Parkinson's disease to depression and anxiety; and wirelessly receive and transmit information so that you won't need a cell phone or a computer to stay in touch.
- Brain surgery will be a thing of the past except in the most severe cases. Advanced neuroimaging will identify mental illness and brain disease before symptoms show and in general be used to "read" minds and predict and control behavior. Microscopic robots—nanobots—will enter your bloodstream to diagnose and repair brain damage. Protein molecules will travel your brain in a similar way to turn on or off brain cells or genes responsible for brain diseases.
- Neuroenhancers from drugs to digital devices will boost memory and mind function in healthy people—and equally powerful drugs will help block painful or traumatic memories. That could mean growing new brain cells to replace neurons damaged by disease or slipping your kids a memory pill while they cram for Advanced Placement calculus.
- Alzheimer's disease, other dementias, and perhaps even mental retardation will be preventable, curable, and even reversible in many people.
- Those who are paralyzed will regain limb and spinal cord function, and thought-driven spare parts will abound, from prosthetic limbs and vision with lifelike function to prosthetic brain chips to store data and perhaps even duplicate neural networks.

Brain Science Is Big Business

This brave new world of brain research is making strange new partners, among them specialized businesses and products.

In fact, it has spawned a whole new industry. Three hot neuro-tech areas that promise major changes in brain research in the near future are neuroimaging, neuropharmacology, and neurodevices such as brain implants. And they are thriving. The *Neurotechnology Industry Report* for 2008 shows 2 billion people worldwide suffering from a brain-related illness, with an annual economic burden of more than $2 trillion. Globally, in 2008, more than 550 public and private companies participated in a neurotech industry where revenues rose 9 percent to $144.5 billion overall, with neuropharmaceuticals reporting earnings of $121.6 billion, neurodevices revenues of $6.1 billion, and neurodiagnostics revenues of $16.8 billion.

The military has a hefty investment in this as well. Neuro-technology and research will help the thousands of soldiers returning from wars with severe brain injuries or missing limbs. Advances will also perfect the toolbox for warfare. Neuroenhancers will keep soldiers and fighter pilots awake and alert for days, and will fine-tune and juice up mental focus and reflexes. Brain-machine interfaces could create new weapons and allow exploration into deep space and other hostile territory. And neuroimaging could allow us to see into brains to predict and possibly control behavior and thoughts.

How Your Brain Works: The Short Version

A refresher on brain basics will help set the context for the detailed chapters that follow.

Your brain is three pounds of flesh, nerves, and fluid that looks like a big walnut but is much softer. Its billion or so specialized cells called *neurons* communicate and form networks through chemicals (especially those called *neurotransmtters*) and minuscule electrical charges that pass over the tiny gaps, or *synapses*, between them.

The overall brain is often described in three parts: the primitive brain, the emotional brain, and the thinking brain.

The *primitive brain*—the brain stem or hindbrain—sits at the top of the spine and takes care of the automated basics, such as breathing, heartbeat, digestion, reflexive actions, sleeping, and arousal. It includes the spinal cord, which sends messages from the brain to the rest of the body, and the cerebellum, which coordinates balance and rote motions, like riding a bike and catching a ball.

Above this, your brain is divided into two similar, but not identical, hemispheres connected by a thick band of fibers and nerves called the *corpus callosum*. Each side functions slightly differently than the other does, and for reasons not yet understood, the messages between the hemispheres and the rest of our body crisscross, so that the right brain controls our left side and vice versa.

The *emotional brain*, or limbic system, is tucked deep inside the bulk of the midbrain and acts as the gatekeeper between the spinal cord and the thinking brain in the cerebrum above. It regulates survival mechanisms such as sex hormones; sleep cycles; hunger; emotions; and, most important, fear, sensory input, and pleasure. The amygdala is our sentry, the hippocampus is the gateway to short-term memory, and the hypothalamus controls your biological clock and hormones, while the thalamus passes along sensory information to the thinking centers in the cortex above. The basal ganglia surround the thalamus, and are responsible for voluntary movement. The so-called pleasure center, or reward circuit, is also based in the limbic system, involving the nucleus accumbens and ventral tegmental area.

The *thinking brain*—the part we usually see when we picture a brain and what is sometimes called the crown jewel of the body—sits on the top, where it controls thoughts, reasoning, language, planning, and imagination. Vision, hearing, speech, and judgment reside here as well.

But let's be honest. In spite of enormous research advances, scientists still have a pretty rudimentary understanding of brain function and how it relates to your thoughts, feelings, and actions. There are frequent announcements about how the sources of some emotions and functions have been "mapped" in the brain, but most of these should be qualified: brain researchers are still trying to figure out much of what goes on between your ears.

But they're gaining on it.

The Way We Were

Here's a quick overview of what we thought then, what we know now, what we will know tomorrow:

Then	Now	Tomorrow
Your brain cells are finite: you have only so many, and they can't be replaced when they die.	Your brain makes new neurons in some areas.	New neurons are created at will, where and when you need them.
Your brain is hardwired, like a machine or computer.	Your brain is changing every second in response to the environment and your mind.	You change and mold your brain as you want and need.
Brain, mind, and body are separate.	Brain, mind, and body are intertwined and inseparable.	Brain, mind, and body are enhanced by machines and computers.
Stroke damage is mostly irreversible and can't be improved after a few months.	Stroke victims can regain functions even years after a stroke with ongoing therapy.	New technologies prevent damage, renew damaged areas, and replace neurons.
Each part of your brain has a specific function.	Your brain is networked, like a village of skilled workers supporting one another.	You direct new brain networks for desired outcomes.
Parkinson's disease and epilepsy are treated with drugs but can't be cured.	Brain implants can stop the tremors of Parkinson's disease and epilepsy.	Proteins or nanobots injected in the bloodstream swim to damaged areas and repair them.

(continued)

Then	*Now*	*Tomorrow*
Memory is accurate and unchanging.	Memory is changeable. Events are "recollected" in a new context and slightly changed.	Memory is manipulated. You can keep the memories you want and erase the ones you don't.
Alzheimer's disease and loss of brain function are inevitable parts of aging.	Active brains retain more function than inactive ones, even in some very elderly people.	Alzheimer's disease is reversible and even curable in many cases.
Surgery is the best way to repair an injured brain.	Noninvasive methods and drugs are preferred to surgery for repairing a brain.	Technology has made surgery obsolete except in the most severe cases.
Environment (nurture) determines mental potential: tabula rasa.	Genetics (nature) determine mental potential: tabula parents.	Epigenetics—nature; nurture; and your own thoughts, feelings, and actions—determine your brain.
Consciousness is a mystery.	Consciousness is a mystery.	Consciousness is a mystery.

CHAPTER ONE

Your Changeable Brain
Neurogenesis, Neuroplasticity, and Epigenetics

IN BRIEF

When you woke up today, you were a new person—literally. Many of the cells in your body had replaced themselves with younger versions, and your brain has been busy as well. Scientists have discovered your brain is a work in process. Every day, it seems, your brain makes new neurons in at least some sections, and almost every second, your brain is changing its networking in response to what you experience, think, feel, and need. In fact, your brain can even direct changes to some of your genes, turning them off or on.

Then: Your brain is hardwired and unchangeable, and you're born with all the brain cells you'll ever have. Good luck, because when they're gone, they're gone.

NOW: Who knew? Your brain creates new neurons in some areas and new networks, even into old age, and it changes physically in response to your actions, thoughts, and emotions. Your genes are not your destiny—or at least not all of it.

Tomorrow: We'll be able to direct changes: stimulate new brain cells and networks where and when we need them; turn genes off and on at will to repair brain damage, restore function, and optimize performance; and rewire our brains to manipulate memory and even reverse dementia and mental retardation.

The revolutionary findings about your brain's remarkable ability to change itself are barely a decade old. Biologists had long believed that the creation of brain cells was completed at or shortly after birth, and that the rest of your life was a slow slide into brain cell loss. In the 1990s, scientists rocked the field of neurobiology with the startling news that the mature mammalian brain is capable of sprouting new neurons in the hippocampus and the olefactory bulbs, and that it continues to do so even into old age. This process is called *neurogenesis*.

Scientists also confirmed what was long suspected: your brain is not hardwired. It can reinvent itself, as it were, by creating new pathways to reroute, readjust, and otherwise change the networking and connections, sometimes even substituting one area for another. When one part of your brain goes south—from a stroke or trauma, for example—other sections can sometimes take over some of those functions. Your brain also changes to reflect what you learn, do, and think. In fact, your brain is physically rearranging its networks just about every minute of every day. That's *neuroplasticity*.

Then they discovered that your actions, thoughts, feelings, or environment can change your genes—more specifically, whether certain genes are expressed—altering brain function; character traits; and risk of some diseases, from cancer to schizophrenia. That's *epigenetics*.

YOUR BRAIN IS A COMPUTER. NO, IT'S A SWISS ARMY KNIFE. NO, WAIT—IT'S THE INTERNET!

Scientists for centuries have focused on the brain in terms of its bits and parts—its components, in tech speak. Some time ago, they saw it as a machine; then, in the century just ended, it was popular to think of the brain as a kind of computer. More recently the Swiss army knife analogy appeared, which seemed to fit with what was being learned as we mapped the brain.

Neuroanatomists figured out that the visual cortex, for example, processes what we see; that Broca's area is the center for language; and that various other areas deal with specific functions and concepts, such as facial recognition, risk taking, romantic love, and even God.

But now it seems that's a bit simplistic too. As we learn more, it has become clear that how well the brain works depends on how these modules are linked together to perform as circuits. The brain is, in fact, more like the Internet.

True, there are areas that specialize. Roughly speaking, reason and rationality happen in the cortical areas, emotion and irrationality are experienced in the limbic system, and a number of interconnected neural networks may be bundled into module-like units. But in most ways, the working of the brain is described today as being splayed out over, under, or through the brain's crevasses—a "distributed intelligence" that more closely matches the World Wide Web.

These extraordinary findings, coupled with new imaging techniques that show the brain in action in real time, opened entire new ways of studying the brain and the tremendous impact of cognition. They showed how neglect, abuse, and bullying in childhood can stunt brain development, and they gave some credibility to age-old concepts of positive personal transformation through religious experiences, meditation, self-help programs, and even positive thinking and your own will. They also explain how and why talking cures such as psychotherapy and cognitive behavior therapy can change lives.

Researchers are working now on ways to both understand and facilitate those changes in beneficial ways. The methods range from some startlingly effective and simple solutions (such as binding back the good limb on a person who has had a stroke so the person is forced to use the affected limb, and the brain is forced to make new pathways) to the most technologically and scientifically complex (such as deep brain implants to block depression, tremors, and convulsions) to brain-machine interfaces and thought-driven prosthetics.

The Birth of Brain Cells: Neurogenesis

We've all heard the warnings: *If you* _____ (fill in the blank) *you'll kill brain cells.* And because scientists believed until very recently that you were born with all the brain cells you'd ever have, that was a fairly dire warning. You broke it, and you were stuck with the results.

Recently we've been able to relax a bit, because we know that our brain makes new cells in at least two sections: the dentate gyrus of the hippocampus, a structure involved in learning and memory, and the olefactory bulbs. And it may in fact create new neurons elsewhere in the brain; we don't know for certain yet.

Most of this research has been done on animals, but some human studies have confirmed the finding. Studies were done on terminal cancer patients who generously agreed to be injected with a marker for new cell production and to offer their brains for study after their death. The autopsies showed that even in the face of aging and death, their brains continued to produce new neurons to the very end.

Chemotherapy could give us an idea of what happens when we don't make new neurons. Chemotherapy impairs the cell division needed for making new cells, and people who have had chemotherapy treatment for cancer and some other serious diseases often complain about a syndrome sometimes referred to as *chemobrain.* They have trouble with the kinds of learning and remembering that everyone finds challenging, such as juggling multiple projects while trying to process new information.

Because having a ready supply of new neurons on tap could help to keep your brain intellectually limber, scientists are looking for ways to exploit this to prevent or treat disorders that bring about cognitive decline. Meanwhile, they've found that these new brain cells disappear if you don't use them.

Changes in Your Brain: Neuroplasticity

Scientists have long known that the brain can change itself. In fact, your brain is probably changing every microsecond in response to experiences, both external and internal. Those changes come mainly from the growth of new connections and networks among neurons, particularly among newborn neurons.

We've known that different kinds of experiences lead to changes in brain structure, with more activity in the networks used most. In musicians, for example, the parts of the brain dedicated to playing their instruments are disproportionately larger than in nonmusicians or in musicians who play a different instrument. A decade-old study of London taxi drivers skilled at navigation in the city center showed the same effect: they had larger hippocampi than nondrivers, reflecting the huge amount of data they needed to have at hand. Moreover, the longer they drove complicated routes around the city, the larger their hippocampi grew.

Also, brains apparently riddled with blank areas or plaque and other signs of Alzheimer's disease have come from people functioning very well into late old age. Indeed, some brains lacking a hemisphere—the entire half of a brain—can function quite well.

We also know the brain can sometimes repair itself after devastating injury, bypassing dead areas to create new connections. ABC news correspondent Bob Woodruff, critically injured by a roadside bomb in 2006 while covering the war in Iraq, suffered a brain injury so severe that part of his skull was permanently removed, and he was kept in a medically induced coma for more than a month. Few believed he would walk again, let alone work as a reporter. After more than a year of intensive therapy, which included relearning speech to

CENTENARIANS RULE: MORE REASONS TO TAKE CARE OF YOUR BRAIN

Centenarians—individuals one hundred years or older—are the fastest growing age group in the United States, and experts predict there may be as many as 1 million by 2050.

If you're sixty years old (or younger) today, you could be in that group. And if you want your mind to be there along with you, take good care of your brain.

You'll have plenty of company near your age: people aged eighty and older are the fastest-growing portion of the total population in many countries. By 2040, the number of people sixty-five or older worldwide will hit 1.3 billion, according to the National Institute on Aging, which announced the figures. And within ten years, there will be more people aged sixty-five and older than children under five in the world for the first time in human history.

The most rapid increase will be in developing countries. By 2040, they will be home to more than 1 billion people aged sixty-five and over—76 percent of the projected world total.

If you reach one hundred years, you are sure to live in interesting times, an old blessing (or curse) of the Chinese (who, incidentally, will have the world's largest population of elders by 2040). This global aging will change the social and economic nature of the planet and present some difficult challenges.

Interesting times, indeed.

overcome aphasia, he made a hard-hitting documentary about the plight of injured soldiers and the deficits in government care. And then he went back to work as a reporter—in Iraq.

Certainly Woodruff benefited from the kind of very expensive and intense treatment not available to all of us. Nevertheless, his recovery shows how remarkably able the brain is, especially because his was not a young brain: he was forty-four at the time of his injury.

What we did not know for certain until recently is that what you think and feel also physically change your brain, such as intellectual challenges, deliberate brain training, anxiety, and joy. So it seems there is a biological basis to mind training: you can learn skills aimed at changing your brain just as you learn repeated activities to change your body. Meditation is a brain-changing example. Studies show that regular practice of meditation results in physical as well as mental and emotional changes. In long-time practitioners of meditation, the two hemispheres become more balanced, the trigger-happy amygdala shows less reaction to emotional sounds, and the many brain regions involved in focused attention show greater activity (see "Boosting Your Brain with Meditation," p. 31).

Changes in Your Genes: Epigenetics

Scientists are finding one of the ways your brain changes itself is by actually changing your genes—or more correctly, by the acting out (or not) of certain genes—in the process of epigenesis.

We know that your genome is the total deoxyribonucleic acid (DNA) that you inherit from your ancestors and contains the instructions for making your unique body and brain. Another layer of information, called the epigenome, is stored in the proteins and chemicals that surround and stick to the DNA. It's a kind of chemical switch that determines which genes are activated (or not): it tells your genes what to do and where and when.

Researchers have discovered that the epigenome can be affected by many things, from aging and diet to environmental toxins to even what you think and feel. This means that even your experiences can literally change your mind by chemically coating the DNA that controls a function. The coating doesn't alter the underlying genetic code; rather, it alters specific gene expression, shutting down or revving up the production of proteins that affect your mental state.

Epigenetics helps explain the gap between nature and nurture that has long puzzled scientists: why some illnesses and traits pop up in one but not both identical twins who have the same DNA, or why these traits skip a generation. It also helps explain neuroplasticity.

One researcher describes DNA as a computer hard disk, with certain areas that are password protected and others that are open. Epigenetics is the programming that accesses that material, writes Jörn Walter of Saarland, Germany, on the Web site Epigenome.

Epigenetics can profoundly affect your health and, it seems, your happiness, changing not only your vulnerability to some diseases such as cancer but also your mental health. Scientists have found, for example, that a mother rat's nurturing, through licking and loving behavior that boosts the expression of a gene that eases anxiety and stress, bolsters emotional resilience in her newborn pups. They've also found that distressing events can turn off the expression of genes for brain cell growth protein and thereby trigger depression, and that epigenetic changes may also underlie the pathology of schizophrenia, suicide, depression, and drug addiction.

The acting-out process of changeable genes—gene expression— is quite complicated and a new area of intense research. Just recently biologists have found that epigenetic changes may be heritable— passed on to your descendants—just as your DNA is. They have also found that altering gene expression with drugs or environments that provide more intellectual stimulation can improve learning and memory in cognitively impaired animals. Future therapies for memory disorders in humans might work in a similar way. It's a promising area with much to be learned. In 2008, the National Institutes of Health invested $190 million in the five-year Roadmap Epigenomics Program to pursue some of these promising fields of research.

Keeping Your New Brain Cells

So it turns out that your brain is a nursery: every day, it seems, new brain cells are born. But it seems that your brain doesn't always keep these newborn neurons. Just like all other babies, they need special care to survive. And it's not pampering: your newborn neurons, scientists are finding, need to be challenged, exercised, and run hard.

If you don't use those new cells, they will disappear. Animal research shows that most of these cells die within a couple of weeks unless that brain is challenged to learn something new and, preferably, something hard that involves a great deal of effort. And *new* is key here as well: just repeating old activities won't support new brain cells.

Scientists still don't really know why or what the heck the new neurons are doing or even why we make them. Are they made to replace dying cells? One theory is that they are backup, produced just in case they are needed. This idea suggests that your brain calls for reinforcements when new brain cells are available to aid in situations that tax the mind, and that a mental workout can buff up the brain much as physical exercise builds up the body.

In animal studies, scientists found that between five thousand and ten thousand new neurons arise in the rat hippocampus every day (it's not known how many we humans make, or how often). The birth rate depends on some environmental factors. Heavy alcohol consumption slows the production, for example, whereas exercise increases it. Rats and mice that log time on a running wheel kick out twice as many new cells as do mice that lead a more sedentary life. Even eating antioxidant-rich blueberries seems to goose the generation of new neurons in the rat hippocampus, as do exciting changes in their cages or new toys to pique their interest.

Elizabeth Gould (a discoverer of neurogenesis in adults), Tracy Stors, and colleagues have been examining the connection between learning and neurogenesis by studying the brains of rats and the importance of hard learning. In their experiments, they first injected the animals with BrdU (bromodeoxyuridine), a drug that marks only brand-new cells. A week later, they recruited half of the treated rats for a training program and let the rest lounge around their home cages.

The rats enrolled in Rodent University were given an eyeblink course: an animal hears a tone and then, some fixed time later (usually 500 milliseconds, or half a second), gets hit in the eye with a puff of air or a mild stimulation of the eyelid, which causes the animal to blink. After several hundred trials, the animal learns to connect the tone with the stimulus, anticipate when the stimulus will arrive, and blink just before that happens: an anticipatory learning based on the ability to predict the future based on what has happened in the past.

After four or five days of training, the scientists found that the rats that had learned to time their blink had also retained more BrdU-labeled neurons (the newborn neurons) in the hippocampus than did rats who were just hanging out in their cages. The animals that got no mental workout held on to only a few of the newborn cells, and animals that failed to learn—or that learned poorly—didn't keep new neurons in spite of the training. Rats that went through some eight hundred trials but never learned to anticipate the eyelid stimulation ended up with just as few new neurons as the slacker animals that never left their cages.

The better the animal learned, the more new neurons it retained, convincing researchers that it was the process of learning—and not simply the exercise of training or exposure to a different cage or a different routine—that rescued new neurons from death.

No Pain, No Gain

Sorry to say, the research also showed that all types of learning are not equal. It seems that learning or practicing easy tasks won't cut it. Keeping new brain cells is like keeping your muscles. You've go to work them hard.

Research, mostly in rats, shows that new neurons that get a workout stay. For example, when rats were put in a pool of water to find and swim to a visible, submerged platform for a safe landing, they didn't keep new brain cells. Scientists speculated that that's because the task didn't require much thought. But when rats had to learn to gauge the time between a sound tone and a stimulus, a much harder problem requiring the ability to predict a future event based on past experience, the neurons survived.

Here's some more good news: the animals that were a bit slow to master the tasks—the plodders and workers—ended up with more new neurons than the fast learners. Scientists assume that means, again, that the more effort, the greater the gain—just like at the gym or when learning calculus.

But the type of workout is important here: crossword puzzles and memory games may not challenge your neurons enough. The puzzles have to be difficult for you, and repeating already-learned skills makes you better at those skills but doesn't apparently improve cognition. It seems the tasks that rescued the most neurons were the ones that are hardest to learn, and that the more engaging and challenging the problem, the greater the number of neurons that stick around. By the way, those can be learning tasks that are fun such as learning to play the violin or rock guitar or how to speak Italian—as opposed to, say, learning inorganic chemistry (unless, of course, inorganic chemistry is fun for you). Anecdotal evidence and some human research have said just the same thing, but so far without the human brain biology to prove it.

Anecdotal accounts suggest that effortful learning may also help some dementia patients. When Stors and colleagues presented her group's animal research at a meeting about Alzheimer's disease and other forms of dementia, the health professionals in the audience were intrigued. They report having seen benefits from such exertions in their patients. And they noted that patients who can fully engage themselves in cognitively demanding activities may be able to delay the progression of this mind-robbing disease.

Brain Training Programs: Help or Hype?

Because studies show brains are like muscles (use it or lose it), many experts are suggesting we do brain training exercises. And many of those experts recommending the exercises are among the producers of cognitive training programs, now a $225 million–plus industry.

Are these sometimes pricey programs as good as exercising your brain on your own (and for free) by playing chess, say, or learning a new language or how to play the mandolin? Possibly not, and if they are, it's hard to say if any one is better than the others. The bulk of the research is murky.

COULD WEIGHT GAIN MAKE YOU A FATHEAD?

Could obesity be bad for your brain? Well, it appears to shrink your gray matter. A section of the Pittsburgh Healthy Women Study looked at weight gains of forty-eight women over an average of fifteen years. Those who had gained the most weight but were completely healthy otherwise showed a decrease in brain gray matter. Scientists conducting the study aren't sure what, if anything, this means, or if being overweight is a cause, but it chalks up one more possible strike against obesity, which by itself raises the risk of brain injury from stroke or heart attack.

And, yes, there's probably a gene for that. In fact, three genes active in the brain have been associated with obesity. If that isn't bad enough, it's also linked to some other bad things. The latest, NRXN3 gene variant, is also associated with alcohol dependence, cocaine addiction, and illegal substance abuse.

Neuroscientist Peter Snyder of Brown University reviewed nearly twenty software studies and concluded that as a group, these training programs were underwhelming. The studies have flaws that induce confounding factors, such as a lack of control groups and follow-up, Snyder warns. In fact, more than a third of those he reviewed were too shoddy even to include in the analysis he published in early 2009 in the journal *Alzheimer's & Dementia*. From his perspective, software companies remain hard-pressed to prove that their products do much, especially over the long term, and few programs have demonstrated the flexibility to boost skills that were not practiced or to increase actual thinking ability. Others have noted that brain programs that involve repetition make you better at repeating that specific task and do not necessarily improve your thinking skills.

Writer Kaspar Mossman sampled a range of programs for *Scientific American Mind*. After eight weeks of testing, he concluded he had learned some useful things about the software but didn't feel any smarter. It could be because he's only in his thirties—not old enough to have any cognitive problems (yet): program developers claim these interactive exercises work best for the brains of people who are having slippage.

If you want to try the programs, what workout works best? You can experiment by taking advantage of the many free trials offered online for these products and see what works for you. What matters most is whether you enjoy using one of these programs, whether it challenges you at the right level, and whether you stick with it.

Or take Synder's advice. The best memory enhancer, he says, is physical exercise, followed by a good diet and an active social life.

Wait. Does that mean reading this book doesn't count?

What's Next? And What About My Brain?

Good questions. So far, we've been looking mostly at animal brains that can be dissected for detailed study.

Scientists are eager to find out how to prompt neurogenesis in human brains—in healthy individuals, as well as in people with brains damaged by Alzheimer's disease, trauma, or stroke. Knowing how neurogenesis works would tell us which treatments, from deep brain stimulation to drugs to gene therapy and stem cell replacement, can best prompt new neurons in the human hippocampus or anywhere else in the brain. We'd also be able to tell if (or which) brain-exercising activities help your physical brain.

They'd also like to know how to better encourage neuroplasticity and understand how to direct epigenesis—to be able to direct some injured brains to make them more nimble and self-healing in cases of mental illness, anxiety, and depression, to help those needing to rewire a brain damaged by autism or a genetic injury, and to learn how to turn genes on and off as needed.

They're mulling many theories and working in many areas of research, spurred and supported by the billions being invested in research on Alzheimer's disease (see "Alzheimer's Disease: The Memory Epidemic," p. 41).

But first researchers need to know more about the basics. Which molecular mechanisms and which neurotransmitters are involved?

Which receptor proteins? And when exactly do those mechanisms operate? Does learning help new neurons to become integrated into neuronal networks, or does it promote the survival of those that are already connected? And how do they do this? Why do we make new brain cells in the first place? And can we prompt the production of extra brain cells to boost healthy brains? It appears that learning promotes the survival of new neurons but does not seem to control the number of new cells produced.

Another important concern will be how to control the amount of neurogenesis a particular treatment prompts, because the overproduction of new neurons can also be dangerous. In some forms of epilepsy, for example, neural stem cells continue to divide past the point at which new neurons can form useful connections. Neuroscientists speculate that these aberrant cells not only end up in the wrong place but also don't mature and could contribute to the miswiring of the brain that causes seizures. So researchers must first better understand the process.

To know (and do) all that, we need better ways to look inside a living human brain without cutting it open. Seeing what goes on in humans when new brain cells are created and exactly how they die or stick around would give tremendous insights into preventing or reversing many brain conditions. Scientists are working toward that with ever more innovative neuroimaging techniques (see "Looking Inside Your Brain," p. 71).

As for helping your brain cells today, lifestyle changes might make the difference, and those might be summed up as brain boosters, butt busters, blueberries, and bliss (see the list of "Six Drug-Free Ways to Boost Your Brain," p. 29). These include challenging mental activities and environments with lots of interesting and stimulating toys; vigorous physical exercise; diets rich in deeply colored vegetables and fruits known to be high in antioxidants and vitamins; and meditation and other calming activities that relieve stress, which is known to be a killer for your new brain cells.

And there's a bonus: all of these are good for the rest of your body as well.

CHAPTER TWO

Boosting Your Brain Power

IN BRIEF

Truck drivers do it. Soldiers do it. Students do it. Even Tibetan monks do it. You'd probably do it too if you aren't already. Humans have been trying to pump up brain power, mental endurance, and emotional balance for thousands of years with an array of ingestibles and mind control practices. So far, there's no "smart pill," though some swear by controversial drugs to treat attention deficit hyperactivity disorder (ADHD). But there's another way to enhance your brain that is time-tested, scientifically proven, has no side effects, is legal, and is free: it's meditation, and it works for millions worldwide.

Then: Animal extracts and herbs were touted to boost brain power. Caffeine, caffeine tablets, and speed kept us awake and aware longer. Recreational drugs, hypnosis, psychedelic music, and transcendental meditation expanded consciousness.

NOW: Black market and off-label use of amphetamine-related ADHD drugs is rampant to sharpen focus, banish sleep, and improve performance. Computerized, online, or other programs touted to improve brain power or memory are big business—but science is showing that meditation and exercise can also improve your brain.

Tomorrow: Your brain will be boosted by safe chemicals, smart molecules, electric stimulation, and brain-implanted computer microprocessors, and by truly effective cognitive programs, including meditation, which will be taught as early as preschool.

The Brave New Pharmacy

There may not be "smart pills" yet, but the psychopharmacy is stocked with some pretty effective drugs that are taking up the slack until the real thing comes along. We're talking about stimulant drugs meant to control ADHD.

Some four million U.S. children have been diagnosed with ADHD, an inability to sustain focused attention, and about half are on some kind of prescribed medication. Millions of adults with ADHD are also on medication. Some have been taking these drugs for decades to help them quell restlessness and improve focus and attention span. People without ADHD are taking these prescription drugs too—in most cases, illegally obtained—hoping to benefit from a boost in focus, extended concentration, and just plain wakefulness to give them a competitive edge in school and work. The black market use is booming, especially among college students who pop them like recreational

BOOSTING YOUR BRAIN POWER

NEED A BOOST? SEND IN THE NOOTROPES

Brain stimulants (so-called) are nothing new. Consider the coca plant, chewed by Incans for millennia for stamina, made into patent medicines and rumored to have been given to soldiers in several wars, and bottled in Coca-Cola in decades past. You've probably used coffee for that morning zip and maybe caffeine pills or drinks or even amphetamines for late-night stay-awakes. Other products—omega-3 oils, ginkgo balboa, St. John's wort, and other herbs—claim to improve your mood, your mind, or your memory.

There's even a term for these (and many other) products purported to improve your mental functions by adjusting your brain's neurochemicals: *noo-trope*, put together from the Greek for *noos* (mind) and *tropein* (to bend).

drugs and boomers in the workforce struggling to keep up with younger, sharper competitors.

Ritalin, Adderall, Provigil, Nuvigil: they've been called "steroids for your brain," and tens of thousands of college students believe it. Surveys suggest that up to 25 percent of students at some colleges and universities are self-medicating to fuel marathon work and study sessions that can last days and give an edge to their test taking. Doctors find patients of all kinds and ages, including other doctors, asking for stimulants in hopes of boosting their productivity. And the military has a keen interest in any drugs that can keep soldiers awake and aware 24/7.

So what's new about this? you may ask, especially if you recall the halcyon drug-hazed days of the sixties. People (and students in particular), you say, have always experimented with recreational drugs. But this is not your daddy's drug of choice, and the effects and intents are quite different. In the sixties, neuroenhancing meant expanded consciousness. Drugs such as LSD, peyote, and pot were taken to mess up the mind a bit and open those doors of perception to creativity and spiritual visions.

Today's neuroenhancing drugs have the opposite aim: they're used to narrow your mind and increase focused attention, mental endurance, and wakefulness. And they aren't taken for fun. They are pragmatically intended to improve your competitive edge, not your spirituality.

Those with an ADHD diagnosis who take these stimulants may achieve that edge. A 2009 study from the University of California at Berkeley's School of Public Health found that kids taking ADHD medication (presumably prescribed) scored better than their ADHD peers who were not medicated. However, they still scored lower than those without ADHD. Studies dating back to the 1970s have shown that children who don't have ADHD also become more attentive after taking stimulants.

The psychopharmacology industry likes these stimulants too. Pharmaceutical firms are pushing awareness of the adult forms of ADHD, and the reason isn't hard to see: prescriptions for methylphenidate and amphetamines rose by almost 12 percent each year between 2000 and 2005, according to a 2007 study, and they are increasing.

Juicing the Brain: The "Smart Drugs"

Most ADHD drugs are a variant on our old friend speed. Among the most popular are the amphetamines methylphenidate (marketed under the name Ritalin) and modafinil (brand name Provigil, an amphetamine developed for narcolepsy); a mixture of amphetamine and dextroamphetamine (Adderall, used to treat narcolepsy and ADHD); and donepezil (Aricept, a cholinesterase inhibitor to boost levels of the neurotransmitter acetylcholine and prescribed for Alzheimer's disease). In 2008, two new stimulants, Vyvanse (amphetamine) and Concerta, received approval from the Food and Drug Administration (FDA) for treating adults.

It hasn't been clear how these drugs calm hyperactivity and boost focus, because amphetamine got its nickname "speed" for a reason.

In fact, public speakers and professional musicians who want to enhance their performance are known to go the other way and take propanolol (Inderal), a beta-blocker that interferes with ephedrine (adrenaline), which can cause jittery nerves and stage fright.

But it appears that the prefrontal cortex and the nucleus accumbens set the stage, and dopamine—the neurotransmitter of good times, addiction, and mood—is a key player. A lack in these areas is common with ADHD.

Those with ADHD typically have an underactive or even smaller-than-average frontal cortex—the brain region that controls so-called executive functions such as decision making, predicting future events, and suppressing emotions and urges. The nucleus accumbens, a critical mediator of motivation, pleasure, and reward, may also be impaired in ADHD.

Dopamine boosts function in both, and less dopamine can mean less mental acuteness. Stimulants such as ADHD drugs (and cocaine; we'll get to that later) enhance communication in these dopamine-controlled brain circuits by binding to the proteins on nerve endings that suck up excess dopamine. Dopamine then accumulates outside the neurons, and this neurotransmitter boost is thought to juice the neuronal circuits critical for motivation and impulse control. The result is a feeling of well-being, confidence, and euphoria that makes everything, including memory, comprehension, and communication, a lot easier. Antidepressants that block the uptake of serotonin, the other feel-good neurotransmitter, work in a similar way to lift depression.

A recent paper in the journal *Biological Psychiatry* that looked at Ritalin suggests that the dosage is crucial. Neuroscientists dosed rats with Ritalin and had them perform the kind of working memory task that daunts those with ADHD. At the same time, they measured neural activity with tiny electrodes implanted in the rats' brains. At low doses, Ritalin primarily affected the prefrontal cortex, jacking up its sensitivity to signals coming in from the hippocampus. And here's how the drug seemed to help with attention: it strengthened choruses of neurons firing together and put a damper on scattered, uncoordinated

"Flowers for Algernon" and *Charly*

Charly, a 1968 movie based on a 1959 short story "Flowers for Algernon," is about a janitor named Charly with an IQ of 68. He undergoes experimental surgery that makes him a near genius and able to best Algernon, a mouse who has undergone similar treatment, in maze testing. The increased intelligence doesn't lead to happiness, though, and it doesn't last. As Charly sees Algernon's new intelligence fade, he perceives his brain boost will also, and he asks scientists to put flowers on Algernon's grave.

activity. But at high doses, the prefrontal cortex tuned out, and Ritalin's effects were similar to those of other stimulants. The rats lost their cognitive edge and became hyperactive, sniffing and licking repetitively. So Ritalin shows that you can indeed have too much of a good thing—to the point of distraction.

The Caveats: Are These Really "Smart Pills"—and Are They Safe?

So far these drugs don't seem to make you smarter or more creative. They do improve recall (for a while), keep you awake longer, and help you focus. Users have said that the pills work best for them when they've decided what needs to be done and embarked on that endeavor. They seem to be most effective for people who are a bit behind the curve, and have less effect on better thinkers—or people with lots of natural dopamine.

They may be affecting younger people differently from their parents, since young brains today tend to live on and in the Internet (see "Are You Born Digital—or a Digital Immigrant?" p. 56). But no one knows yet how long-term use of these enhancers affects the brain. College-age and older users of off-label ADHD drugs don't express much concern: after all, they grew up watching their class-mates with ADHD take these pills for a decade or more with no per-ceived ill effects.

It's true that millions of people have taken these medications without obvious incident since they were first prescribed in the 1950s, and a number of studies have found no adverse effects on stimulant-treated children or even differences between stimulant-treated chil-dren and those not on medication. In 2009 child psychiatrist Philip Shaw of the National Institute of Mental Health and his colleagues used MRI scans to measure the change in the thickness of the cerebral cortex (the outer covering of the brain) of forty-three youths between the ages of twelve and sixteen who had ADHD. The researchers found no evidence that stimulants slowed cortical growth. In fact, only the unmedicated adolescents showed more thinning of the cerebrum than was typical for their age, hinting that the drugs might facilitate normal cortical development in young people with ADHD.

But—and there's always a but—there's animal evidence and growing concern that long-term use might take a toll on the brain. Human studies show that areas of the brain that govern growth in children taking these medications are affected. In addition, a smat-tering of recent animal studies hints that stimulants could alter the structure and function of the brain in ways that may depress mood; boost anxiety; and, contrary to short-term effects, lead to cognitive deficits.

In February 2007, the FDA issued warnings about side effects such as growth stunting and psychosis, among other mental disorders. The mental issues could be due more to ADHD than the pills, but it's a chicken-or-egg kind of conundrum. Having ADHD is a risk factor for other mental problems. The vast majority of adults with ADHD have at least one additional psychiatric illness—often an anxiety disorder or drug addiction. Does use of stimulants in childhood con-tribute? They do, after all, activate the brain's reward pathways, which are part of the neural circuitry that controls mood under normal conditions.

Moreover, the addiction issue is a specter for the long-term use of any drug that mucks with your brain's reward circuitry. Methylphenidate has a chemical structure similar to that of cocaine (we promised we'd be getting to cocaine) and acts on the brain in a similar way. Both cocaine and methamphetamine (also called "speed" or "meth") block dopamine transporters to increase the effect, just as ADHD drugs do. In cocaine, the dopamine surge is so sudden it makes users high, as well as unusually energetic and alert.

Recent experiments in animals have sounded the alarm that methylphenidate may alter the brain in ways similar to cocaine. In February 2009 neuroscientists Yong Kim and Paul Greengard, along with their colleagues at Rockefeller University, reported cocaine-like structural and chemical alterations in the brains of mice given methylphenidate.

Amphetamines such as Adderall could alter the mind in other ways. A team led by psychologist Stacy A. Castner of the Yale University School of Medicine has documented long-lasting behavioral oddities, such as hallucinations, and cognitive impairment in rhesus monkeys that received escalating injected doses of amphetamine over either six or twelve weeks.

Still, although studies hint that these drugs stunt growth in humans, other human studies haven't shown harm from taking ADHD medications as prescribed. Whether the drugs alter the human brain in the same way they alter that of certain animals is unknown for many reasons, not the least of which is that the brains of different species may vary in sensitivity to stimulant medications.

Nevertheless, a 2009 study suggested a link between ADHD drugs and sudden death in children and teens, with medicated children six to seven times more likely to die suddenly. Although the study methodology is debatable (information on ADHD-medicated children came from interviews with parents and doctors years after the deaths), it raised uneasiness among parents, and it should raise an alarm among those without ADHD who are taking the drugs. There are some ethical issues as well (see "Mental Doping on the Rise: They Jail Athletes, Don't They?" p. 137).

Six Drug-Free Ways to Boost Your Brain

The future will no doubt deliver ever better ways to make our brains sharper and smarter. You won't have to wait long—but why wait at all? Here are some old-fashioned tried-and-true methods that will give your brain a boost without medication.

#1 Exercise It

Physical exercise without a doubt may be the best thing you can do for your brain. It improves the delivery of oxygen and nutrients to brain cells, helps spawn neurons in the hippocampus, and lowers your risk of dementia as neurons (and you) age.

In fact, seniors who work out have better executive function than those who are sedentary. Even seniors who spent their entire lives on the couch can improve their golden years just by starting to move more. Studies have shown that as little as twenty minutes of walking a day can do the trick.

Research has also shown that exercise can increase levels of a substance called brain-derived neurotrophic factor (BDNF), which encourages growth, communication, and survival of neurons and improves sleep quality.

"Of course, all this research does nothing to help explain dumb jocks," Emily Anthes wrote in *Scientific American Mind*. Maybe you have to have a brain to start with?

#2 Feed It Fat

Your brain is mostly fat and needs fat for fuel. But the wrong kind can help you lose your mind: saturated fats are no better for the brain than for the body, and they seem to increase the risk for dementia along with clogged arteries.

Omega-3 fats, however, may lower that risk and pump up brain power. Alzheimer's disease, depression, schizophrenia, and central nervous system disorders may be associated with low levels of omega-3 fatty acids. Omega-3s are found in fatty fish (wild, not farmed), nuts and seeds, and that old standby, cod liver oil. Other superfoods are colorful fruits and vegetables; they are high in antioxidants, which may counteract atoms that can damage brain cells.

If you really want to play with diet, eating less overall also improves brain function—in rats, at least.

#3 Stimulate It

Learn something new and hard. It seems that your brain makes new neurons quite often, but if you don't give them a good workout and something interesting to do, they die. A significant percentage of better-brain wannabes are stimulating their brains with speed: amphetamine drugs developed for ADHD or narcolepsy. Cocaine has similar effects but is less benign, not to mention illegal. Learning Mandarin Chinese or how to play chess might be a better bet and won't have any unwanted side effects. Or jail time. There are lots of other challenges: take up the violin, design a vacation cabin, build a canoe from scratch, or try something fun you've always wanted to do but have been postponing for years.

#4 Play with It

Consider another form of stimulation: playing video games, which research has shown can improve mental dexterity, hand-eye coordination, pattern recognition, attention spans, and information-processing skills. But not all video games, a $10 billion industry in the United States, are benign. Studies show gamers had patterns of brain activity consistent with aggression while playing first-person shooter games. Men show more activity in the brain's reward circuitry when playing and are more than twice as likely as women to say they feel addicted to video games.

New research, however, hints that surfing the Net ups mental activity in older adults.

#5 Serenade It

That highly publicized "Mozart effect" study that suggested listening to classical music could boost cognitive performance has been pretty much discredited. Nevertheless, playing or listening to music does create good vibrations in your brain, from better moods to better sleep, and can activate your brain's reward centers and depress activity in the amygdala, reducing fear and other negative emotions. That may lower stress and thus help your brain keep those new neurons, which are cut dead by stress. It also lowers blood pressure and thus the risk of stroke.

#6 Meditate It

Scores of studies are showing that the ancient practice of meditation seems to help all types of conditions—anxiety disorders, pain, high blood pressure, asthma, stress, insomnia, diabetes, and depression—and boosts the immune system. That's quite a bonus for sitting quietly an hour or less a day. Meditation also physically changes your brain in good ways. Long-time meditators have a thicker cerebral cortex, particularly in regions associated with attention and sensation. Their brain cells tend to fire in synchrony, which relates to better function, and there's more activity in the parts of the prefrontal cortex associated with positive emotions like happiness.

Boosting Your Brain with Meditation

It's legal, freely available; has no side effects; and is proven to enhance clarity of thought and focus, along with compassion, happiness, and inner peace. It's practiced in almost every culture and it's available everywhere, anytime, at no cost. Wait—that's not completely true: Meditation that changes your brain (and possibly your life) takes practice, preferably daily practice, of twenty minutes or more.

And there are studies to prove these benefits. Meditation has been shown to increase immunity, lower pulse and respiration, even out activity in the two hemispheres of the brain, and make your thinking and remembering brain larger. The brains of meditators are thicker in areas related to focused attention and sensory data processing (the prefrontal cortex and right anterior insula). And studies funded by the National Institutes of Health are under way that may show more about how meditation can change and enhance your brain.

WHAT IS MEDITATION?

Meditation is an ancient practice to increase awareness and help focus and quiet the mind and body. It is not necessarily spiritual or religious and is practiced worldwide by millions, with or without religious overtones.

Basically it involves sitting quietly and being aware without becoming involved in your thoughts and emotions as they arise. When the mind wanders, it is gently returned to the object of focus. Although there are many different techniques and methods, they all fall more or less into two groups: focused attention and open monitoring.

In focused attention, the meditator brings the mind to focus on a single thought, phrase, object, or idea without becoming caught up in other thoughts or emotions that arise. Many practices use this. In Zen, the meditator may focus on a koan, a riddle posed by the teacher; in transcendental meditation (TM), the meditator focuses on and silently repeats a mantra (a Sanskrit phrase). In other practices, attention focuses on the breath or on a deity.

Open monitoring meditation is often practiced after training with focused attention. It involves no specific point of focus but rather an increasing awareness (or mindfulness) of the physical environment, and of thoughts and emotions as they arise, without reaction or judgment.

Some meditation methods include simple breathing and relaxation techniques.

Although practiced for millennia in the East, meditation was virtually unknown in Western countries until the 1960s, when the Beatles took up with Indian guru Maharishi Mahesh and began practicing a kind of meditation called TM. Movie stars and other celebrities followed, prompting a wave of idealistic young visitors who flocked to spiritual centers (ashrams) in India and the creation of such centers throughout the United States.

Most scientists regarded this as New Age spiritual nonsense until studies began showing that meditating lowered blood pressure; respiration; and levels of cortisol, the stress neurotransmitter. Harvard University professor Herbert Benson, founder of the Mind/Body Medical Institute, further legitimized meditation when he wrote about the practice in nonspiritual terms in the 1975 book *The Relaxation Response*.

Since then, meditation has become increasingly part of the mainstream medical and scientific community. It's the core of a stress reduction program initiated by long-time meditator Jon Kabat-Zinn that is offered at hundreds of medical centers, hospitals, and health maintenance organizations, including the California HMO giant Kaiser Permanente.

It is taught with great success in some prisons, where it helps inmates control emotions and cope with the stresses of prison life; and in some public elementary schools, where, some studies show, it boosts concentration and harmony and even improves grades.

The increase in focused attention could also improve understanding in face-to-face relationships and perhaps help those who suffer from abnormal emotional reactions, says Paul Ekman, a noted expert in facial expressions and emotion and professor emeritus of psychology at the University of California, San Francisco. Ekman found that lamas assessed the emotion shown in others' faces much faster and more accurately than did "thousands of people I have tested over the years, including lawyers, policemen, and judges."

The NIH has been very interested in this work. Over the past twenty years, it has granted more than $24 million to study the effects of the TM program and related programs on cardiovascular disease, and has found that regular practice can lower high blood pressure and reduce arteriosclerosis—circulatory conditions that contribute to strokes and other brain damage.

Meditation Means Changing Your Brain

The current wave of scientific interest in meditation was spurred in part by cooperation from the Dalai Lama, the exiled leader of Tibet and arguably the world's best-known spiritual leader. He has had a lifelong interest in science and has been holding regular seminars with some of the world's most distinguished scientists focused on relieving human suffering and working toward world peace.

He made it possible for researchers to look at the brains of some of the world's longest-term meditators: monks often living in isolation in Tibet who have been meditating for decades. Images and recordings of the brain activities of these master meditators have revealed much about the effects of meditation on the brain, especially when compared to nonmeditators.

Richard Davidson of the University of Wisconsin, Madison, is among Western scientists studying meditation with the cooperation of the Dalai Lama and $6 million in NIH grants. Davidson, a professor of psychology and psychiatry who practices meditation, was one of the first to record the brain activity of Tibetan monks during their altered state. His team has since conducted several creative experiments to test the possible neural benefits and changes, including how electrical brain activity corresponds to emotional and behavioral reactions to the environment. He has shown that meditation triggers the high-frequency waves associated with attention and perception to a far greater degree in experienced practitioners than in novices.

To Davidson, meditation is an outstanding example of neuro-plasticity and enhancement. "The brain is the organ built to be changed by experience and modulated by training," he says. "The benefits are within the reach of all of us."

But although he has been studying some who have been meditating for decades, Davidson says it doesn't take that long for a meditation practice to begin to change your brain. Changes in the brain occur every microsecond, he reminds us: "How long it takes people to notice a change depends on how sensitive they are to changes. Data show one can observe changes with periods of practice as short as two weeks."

Meditation is increasing in the United States among people who have no interest in the spiritual aspects, but who are finding it provides relief from stress, chronic pain, and anxiety with as little as twenty minutes of daily practice.

The style or type of meditation appears to matter in the sense that different brain circuits are activated by different meditation practices, Davidson says. But this work is in the embryonic stage. A lot more research is required to show this and much more about the very real biological impact of meditation.

What's Next? And What About My Brain?

Wherever you fall on the ethical issues, brain-boosting medication will be in wide use as soon as it becomes legally (and more easily) available. With the virtually guaranteed payback, pharmaceutical companies are most likely at this very moment devising something even bigger and better for your brain power (and more lucrative for them).

There will be other options too. In the future, a shock to the brain from electricity delivered in deep brain stimulation (DBS) via an implanted electrode may boost brain performance by prompting the creation of more neurons, balancing hemispheres, or stimulating creativity. Magnetic charges delivered from outside the skull might be fine-tuned to have similar effects. Information might be downloaded in a similar way by electrodes or microchips in the brain (see "Your Bionic Brain," p. 101).

But as research shows, one of the more effective and noninvasive ways of boosting your brain may come from something you can do yourself: meditation and mental and physical exercises. We know that more than drugs change and boost the brain: our thoughts and actions have a powerful effect. More hard-nosed research will be needed, but neuroscience is beginning to accept the tremendous impact of mind techniques such as meditation.

But, you may be thinking, what does this have to do with my brain? I don't live in a serene monastery. Well, in Tibet, in India, and in many other cultures, meditation is not reserved for secluded practitioners: it's part of daily practice. In China, millions every day do Tai Chi, which has a strong meditative component.

Richard Davidson compares it to the1950s, when few people regularly exercised. Today most people in Western countries accept the idea that physical exercise is good for health, and a substantial number incorporate it into their daily routines. It's no different for mental exercise, says Davidson: once people begin to understand the benefits, mental practices will be regarded in the same way as physical exercise.

He and other neuroscientists studying meditation foresee a time when mental exercises such as meditation will be taught in the classroom, beginning with preschool or kindergarten, to make them a lifelong habit and help children learn how to quiet mind and body, focus thoughts, and control emotions.

CHAPTER THREE

Manipulating Your Memory

IN BRIEF

Memory is essential for survival, functioning, and our very identity. We need memory to create our sense of self, and (some think) immortality is the memory of you that is held by others. No wonder losing memory is one of the tragedies of Alzheimer's and other diseases of dementia. But sometimes memory is the enemy. Trauma, pain, and horror can be so deeply encoded in memory that it cripples. Research promises to help fix both: In the coming decades, we may be able to guide our brains to remember what we need and want and to forget what we don't.

Then: Memory is fixed, accurate, and unchangeable, and may be accessed with the right techniques—unless it has been lost in dementia. Then nothing can be done.

NOW: Memory is unreliable, changing with age and with shifts in brain chemistry and neural networks. Animal research shows it's possible to cement or erase some memories, but there's no cure or effective treatment for Alzheimer's disease.

Tomorrow: Scientists will have unraveled the mechanisms and mysteries of how humans make and keep memories and be able to manipulate specific memories, stop or reverse Alzheimer's disease, and even boost cognitive function in those who are mentally disabled. Brain implants may also enlarge our memory storehouse.

Memories Are Made of This—We Hope

Let's see: What was that address? When am I due at that appointment? Who is that woman who just said hello? And where, oh where, are my car keys?

Most of the time, it seems that memory is all about the past. But in fact, memory is about the present and the future, helping us move through the now. It's the process of acquiring and storing information from our experiences that we will need for navigating similar situations in the future. Our very survival may depend on it.

But a good memory is a gift and a curse. Memory can enhance our present experiences with overlays of joy and good times recollected. Unfortunately, we can also be jerked all too vividly into an unpleasant memory from the past—one you'd like to forget: the moment of terror right before the car crash, the incredible pain afterward, the face of a rapist or mugger, your wracking guilt at failing to catch your toddler as she fell down the stairs.

Soon, neuroscientists say, you may be able to manipulate memory. Researchers are making astounding breakthroughs in understanding and being able to change what our brains keep. Here's what we might expect in a few decades:

- Readily available medications to boost short-term and cement long-term memories
- Biochemical treatments to stop and reverse Alzheimer's disease and allow us to retrieve lost memories
- Gene manipulation to improve memory and learning in injured brains and even in those brains born mentally disabled
- Brain-implanted microchips or microprocessors to store information, including complex data we might not need to access every day
- Ways to erase, or stop from being consolidated, specific painful and disturbing memories

How Memory Works—the Short Version

It's tempting to think of memories as bits of specific information stored in a specific place, rather like love letters in an old shoebox, that you can just retrieve at will.

However, your memories are not held neatly inside molecules or neurons. Instead, they are created when messages are sent across the tiny gaps between neurons called synapses, from the outgoing axon on one neuron to the receiving dendrite on another. A memory is held in the connections made by this network and firmly established when a network of synapses is strengthened—temporarily for a short-term memory and permanently for a long-term one. Over time, this net of memories can be strengthened further, weakened, or broken, depending on your brain chemistry, your genes, and your actions.

"We are our memories," said Joseph LeDoux, a professor of neural science and psychology at New York University and a leader in research on emotion, fear, and memory. "One of the big mysteries is how memory makes us who we are. We'll understand it better, and come to terms with how memory is potentiated in the brain, and how it is processed in different systems: We don't understand yet how those systems interact."

Scientists have long puzzled over why and how we choose to retain some but not other information. Your brain is constantly filtering incoming messages, deciding what information to keep and how to go about it. Sometimes it takes repetition—for example, to learn that 6 × 7 is 42, memorize the Periodic Table of Elements, or learn the birthdays of all your relatives. And sometimes, says memory researcher R. Douglas Fields, we don't need to be told twice. A single potent experience can burn an experience indelibly into your brain, and that's never more true than when the memory is connected with survival.

Fields, chief of the section on nervous system development and plasticity at the National Institute of Child Health and Human Development, has been studying memory making for years and writing about it for *Scientific American*. He gives this example of a childhood memory that persists. There's a shortcut to school that crosses the old Dugan place, which is overgrown with weeds and littered with junk cars. Just as you set foot on the property, Old Man Dugan throws open his screen door and two pit bulls charge, snarling with teeth bared. You run for your life, narrowly escaping. The next morning and forever after, you take the long route. When you return years later to that place, your heart still races, even though Dugan and his dogs are long gone.

In the years since the incident, you have developed a lifelong phobia of dogs. Why? Because, Fields says, from a biological or evolutionary perspective, memory is about the future. It keeps only what you need. There's no survival value in having a recording system in the brain that accurately retains every event and experience. (Anyone struggling to manage burgeoning e-mail files knows the solution is not a bigger inbox: it's to delete the files that won't be needed.)

The trick for your brain is to weigh the minute-to-minute experiences and instantly pick out the ones to keep for reference and the ones to discard. Now the survival value of certain events is immediately apparent, and memories of them are socked away permanently. After the Dugan episode, Fields says, you'll always recognize the danger in the presence of an onrushing dog.

Alzheimer's Disease: The Memory Epidemic

Forgetting is also part of memory. Alzheimer's disease is the nine-hundred-pound gorilla in the living room: you can't do much about it, but you can't ignore it either, and you don't know when, or if, it will turn on you.

An estimated 36 million people worldwide have dementia of some kind; of that number, 5.3 million in the United States have Alzheimer's disease. Nearly half of everyone over the age of eighty-five develops dementia, and the numbers will swell as boomers enter old age. By 2050, an estimated 100 million people worldwide will have dementia. Some people who carry a certain genetic risk factor may start memory loss as early as their mid-fifties.

Neuroscientists (whose brains are also at risk) are on the job looking for ways to preserve what we have, prevent more decline, and reverse damage from disease or trauma. They are seeking the mysteries of memory. Billions are being spent on this research: more than $148 billion a year is spent overall on people with Alzheimer's disease, and an estimated $1 billion alone is spent yearly on treatments that have limited effect, if any. Much of that is Medicare money.

Until recently, it was thought that dementia was an inevitable and normal part of aging, with no treatment and no cure. But the near future holds real promise that Alzheimer's disease and other dementias will be detected early on, be preventable, be treatable, or even be reversible in some people. Researchers are working on some exciting and novel therapies, including a chemical switch to manipulate genes, a vaccine against it, drugs to stop or reverse mental deterioration, and even computer chip brain implants to supplement memory. The Alzheimer's Disease Neuroimaging Initiative, the largest Alzheimer's disease study ever funded by the National Institutes of Health, has researchers at fifty-nine centers looking for ways to predict early onset of the disease.

In *Rainbows End*, a science-fiction novel set in 2025, the main character had wasted away with Alzheimer's disease for years, and at age seventy-five has just been cured by newly developed treatments that completely reversed his symptoms. Today's research is advancing so fast that a treatment, if not such a reversal, may be possible by that date.

Researchers are investigating the reasons for memory loss, with new findings about how Alzheimer's disease chews up the brain. The German doctor it's named for found senile plaques in the brain composed of beta-amyloid protein and a slew of other toxins, forming a poisonous gunk that kills cells. Today there is speculation that soluble beta-amyloid (in the form of particles too small to see with the eye), rather than the clumpy plaques, interferes with synaptic signaling and memory and weakens neurons.

But some researchers are wondering now about the role of the beta-amyloid. Is it perhaps the result rather than the cause of Alzheimer's disease? Autopsies reveal that 40 percent of people who performed very well up until death with no symptoms of Alzheimer's disease have amyloid-gunked-up brains.

They speculate now that Alzheimer's disease is caused not only by damaged neurons and a declining number of neurons—apparently people with the disease do continue to produce some new brain cells—but also by a problem in making good connections among the neurons. Some think oxidative stress contributes by damaging brain cells: this is the wear and tear caused when the body can't dispose of excess reactive oxygen (or free radicals), the molecules that are a byproduct of our daily metabolism.

Meanwhile, researchers are finding ways to predict Alzheimer's disease early on when treatments may be more effective. Researchers at the Memory Disorders Clinic at the University of California at San Diego Medical Center have developed a fully automated procedure, volumetric MRI, that measures the "memory centers" in the brains of aging volunteers and compares them to expected size. The process may predict when mild cognitive impairment is likely to progress to Alzheimer's disease and signal a need for aggressive therapy. Because it's automated, the program doesn't require a highly trained (and highly expensive) expert. It could be used for screening in any clinic that has the software.

What We Know Now About Dementia

Your brain has a better chance of avoiding dementias if you have picked your ancestors well and if you've led (and continue to lead) a physically and intellectually active life, with moderate indulgence in alcohol and/or marijuana, which, it seems, can help some people.

Research finds that many promising treatments for Alzheimer's disease don't work, among them omega-3 oils, Vitamin E, and daily use of nonsteroidal anti-inflammatory drugs (NSAIDs).

But some other surprising things do. A small circle of friends or one friend with whom there is a close relationship, even if it's a caregiver, has been shown to be as effective as some drugs in offsetting the effects of Alzheimer's disease. We already know that controlling hypertension by lowering blood pressure (with drugs, diet, exercise, or all three) is connected with a lower risk of Alzheimer's disease. Some ACE (angiotensin-converting enzyme) inhibitors may lower Alzheimer's risk while they are lowering blood pressure, because they cross the blood-brain barrier and lower inflammation in the brain. Other studies show that ACE is a good enzyme because it inhibits beta-amyloid proteins.

Antidepressants help people with Alzheimer's cope (and help their families cope as well) and may slow the progress of dementia. A study in 2007 found that chronic treatment with antidepressants increases daily living and global functioning in patients with Alzheimer's—a hint, at least, that such therapy might promote the production and survival of new neurons in healthy brains as well.

The Indian spice curcumin (turmeric) has been shown not only to prevent the formation of amyloid plaques but to stop the progression in test tube studies and in mice. Combined with Vitamin D_3, it appears to work even better. Studies also found that cinnamon inhibited the growth of abnormal tau, the brain tangles that are a hallmark of Alzheimer's disease.

There could be a golden years lining in the clouds for elders with leukemia and other serious immune diseases who were treated with intravenous immunoglobulin (IVIg): a study that analyzed the medical records of 847 people given at least one treatment of IVIg over four years and 84,700 who were not given IVIg found those who were treated had a 42 percent lower risk of developing Alzheimer's disease.

Drinking coffee and alcohol, of all things, is also linked with lower risk of Alzheimer's disease in mice. Two studies in the July 2009 *Journal of Alzheimer's Disease* with mice bred to develop the disease show caffeine significantly decreased levels of proteins connected with the disease. The alcohol finding is especially interesting because large amounts of alcohol kill your brain. A Wake Forest University Baptist Medical Center study compared teetotalers with light, moderate, and heavy drinkers over a six-year period. They found that moderate drinkers (eight to fourteen drinks per week) who started the study with no cognitive problems were 37 percent less likely to develop Alzheimer's disease compared to abstainers. Those who had some mild cognitive loss or were heavy drinkers had a faster decline.

But the biggest surprise is the potential benefit of pot.

Marijuana to Ward Off Alzheimer's? Wow. Like, Cool.

Marijuana is infamous for its ability to muddle thoughts and dull reactions, and that's the reason some people love it so. But researchers in labs around the world are finding the wicked weed may do the opposite for those with Alzheimer's disease. It may blunt the progression of the disease perhaps even more successfully than the most frequently prescribed medications. Ironically, they discovered this action while looking for a vaccine against pot.

We know the neurotransmitter acetylcholine and the cholinergic neurons that make it are key to forming memories. Researchers found that drugs that block the breakdown of these slow the progression of Alzheimer's disease, although they may offer too little too late. Often by the time Alzheimer's disease has been diagnosed, too much of the brain has been destroyed. Preventing the disease at an earlier stage may be the best bet for those predisposed to the disease.

Research is showing that the psychoactive ingredient in marijuana, tetrahydrocannabinol (THC), may outperform cholinesterase inhibitors and prevent the breakdown of these essential neurochemicals, and may also keep the plaque from forming. As researchers continue, they are finding other chemical benefits from pot in the brain.

Cannabinoids, for example, occur naturally in the human body as well as in marijuana. The notion that cannabinoids derived from marijuana can help Alzheimer's disease patients has its critics. The drug is illegal, and it's not benign: smoking it contributes to several kinds of cancers, much as smoking tobacco does, and marijuana has been shown to contribute to confusion, anxiety, and psychotic symptoms.

So experts don't recommend taking up toking in elder years. But if you happen to have used pot in your past, it could be that that might help your brain out now. Further studies, and your memory, will tell.

Making Memories Stick Around

This is what we want: to be able to remember which woodland plant is poisonous, the password to our most sensitive computer files, every detail of that wonderful vacation in Rome, and where we put the keys (always those darn keys).

There's a complication, however, and it has to do with the ephemeral quality of chemistry. The human brain contains more than 100 billion neurons; the axons of one neuron can be surrounded by 10 to 100,000 dendrites from which it must choose when creating a memory network. And it has to do it quickly. The new proteins needed to cement the memory must be synthesized in the neural networks within minutes of an experience for it to be coded in memory. Then it determines if it will be permanent.

But all proteins in the body break down and are replaced constantly over a period of hours or days. Scientists have known since the 1960s that proteins are needed to strongly cement the network of synapses to make memories stick around, and that genes tell cells to produce proteins. So turning on specific genes was somehow involved in making memories permanent.

To strengthen a neural connection for a lifetime, some other process must also take place to bolster the physical structure of a synapse or to form additional synapses between these neurons. In Alzheimer's disease, for example, it's these connections that are somehow broken or can't form anew to create memories of recent events.

That transition from temporary to permanent memory is called *consolidation*, and it benefits from just the right amount of short-term stress or excitement. The stronger the incoming data to your brain—the more times the data are repeated and the more intense or emotional the message—the stronger and longer lasting the memory. Other challenging experiences such as mastering hard-to-learn tasks strengthen these connections. That's why you recall your most intense past experiences so vividly in the present. Any experience that sparks passion, any situation that is truly novel, anything you put in your mouth that tastes extremely foul or delicious—each of these has a high probability of being remembered as an event important for the future.

Not surprisingly, fear is a powerful memory maker. (Remember those pit bulls?) Neuroscientists have discovered that a rush of epinephrine (adrenaline) releases a flood of stress hormones and neurotransmitters that activate the amygdala, your brain's center for fear and emotion and fight or flight. The amygdala connects to many other regions where different kinds of memories are stored, and it boosts the incoming information that has emotional impact. Consolidation therefore can possibly be aided by increasing levels of these neurotransmitters or hormones. But too much (or constant) stress has the opposite effect.

This chemical action, by the way, is the basis for the action of some memory-enhancing drugs such as the ADHD drugs used illicitly by healthy people to boost concentration—and, of course, for the mild, temporary, (and legally) cognitive-enhancing effects of caffeine or nicotine.

In the future, better drugs may help better preserve memories. Neuroscientists are looking at chemicals to turn off and on genes and at enzymes and proteins to mold memory. There's much new research into the chemistry of memory making. At Wake Forest University School of Medicine, researchers recently have discovered that protein complexes called proteasomes in brain cells may be involved in manipulating memory. Proteasomes control levels of protein and may decrease the strength of messages sent across synapses among neurons.

Similarly, chemicals can help erase bad memories altogether.

A MEMORY TRICK FROM THE LAB

We all know from trying to remember people's names when we first meet them that repetition is necessary to move the name from short-term into long-term storage. And we have our memory tricks. Some people, for example, can remember a name better if they say and hear it out loud, so there's an aural connection. Others like to write a name down and look at it, which is more visual. But scientists have discovered another process that could make it easier.

Neuroscientists attempting to understand memory networks have studied animal brains and measured the effects of neurotransmitters, the chemical molecules that carry messages across the synapse. Looking at how long the message endures, they've found the synapse remains stronger for several hours after a short series of stimuli (in this case, mild electrical shocks), and then the voltage produced by the synapse slowly subsides to its original level. But if three consecutive shocks are delivered to the mice at about ten-minute intervals, the synapse becomes permanently strengthened.

So it appears that repeating the person's name (the stimulus for you) three times right after you are introduced won't help as much in remembering as repeating the name to yourself every ten minutes. This makes sense in evolutionary terms, as a stimulus encountered repeatedly over time is more likely to be important.

Erasing Bad Memories: A Morning-After Pill for the Brain

There are plenty of reasons to want to forget: severe trauma and major life accidents, the death of loved ones, abuse, the horrors of war.

Post-traumatic stress disorder (PTSD) keeps painful memories fresh for half of those who are raped and nearly 20 percent of those who have been in serious vehicular accidents. The PTSD aftermath still affects victims of 9/11, Hurricane Katrina, and the Gulf War, and thousands of wounded warriors are returning from Iraq with psychic as well as physical wounds. The suicide rate among veterans is at an all-time high—the highest since the military began keeping records three decades ago, reports the *New York Times*.

But it doesn't take a major trauma for us to seek forgetfulness. It can be a humiliation in school or at work; a lost opportunity or cherished keepsake; or a broken relationship, as in the film *Eternal Sunshine of the Spotless Mind*, in which the estranged lovers have the memories of their affair erased. Or erasing memories could be a convenient tool for government agents to relieve the citizenry of inconvenient memories, as in the 1997 science-fiction film *Men in Black*.

Indeed, our actions show that many of us have something we are yearning to forget. Why else do we drink, smoke pot, turn to heroin and tranquilizing drugs? We want to muddle up, and perhaps block out, some of the stuff in our brains, suggests noted neuroscientist and psychobiologist Michael S. Gazzaniga. It's why he thinks that the average adult would choose not to go for memory enhancers or black market use of ADHD drugs. Most of us have adjusted over the years to our own individual level of remembering and forgetting. Changing that setting could upset our daily lives and our own personal narratives.

In the worst case, enhancing memory might bring back the unpleasant memories of a bad experience we won't then be able to forget again.

Eternal Sunshine of the Spotless Mind

A two-year love affair ends badly, and the lovers (played by Jim Carrey and Kate Winslet in this 2004 film) decide separately to have their memories of each other erased. A business specializing in memory erasure obliges, but afterward (and after many plot changes) the former lovers meet again as strangers and inexplicably find themselves drawn to each other and reunite.

Erasing memory isn't new, but being able to erase exactly, and only, what we want to get rid of would be. We've been able to erase memory for decades with electroshock therapy (EST), at least temporarily (though indiscriminately and sometimes brutally). But EST doesn't affect consolidated memories. The same is true of a trauma during the consolidation phase, such as a blow to the head or an accident that disrupts brain activity and leaves a gap in memory for that period of time—but doesn't help erase those old, set, terrible memories.

Neuroscientists are working toward finding something better and more precise. Think of it as a morning-after pill for your brain: a treatment specific to a recent group of traumatic memories, given within hours or days of the incident, and preventing the memory from becoming set.

Researchers are working on many different approaches. Most involve manipulation of the brain's chemistry—not surprising, since more than one hundred molecules are known to be involved in some way in making memory. The experiments have been done with rodents, which are first taught to fear a certain stimulus and then given a therapy that makes them "forget" their fear (or behave as if they forgot, as we really don't know what rodents are thinking).

But remember that we need to know the past to survive in the present and future, so it could be dangerous to do away with some memories.

Men in Black

In this 1997 romp, agents Kay and Jay, played by Tommy Lee Jones and Will Smith, are members of a top-secret organization established to monitor and police alien activity on earth. Over the course of the movie, they upset an intergalactic plot and prevent the destruction of the earth. And then they use flashy little devices called neuralyzers to wipe witnesses' memories of events and replace them with benign memories.

Neuroscientists are closing in on erasing memory. At the University of Toronto in Canada, researchers selectively targeted neurons that are involved in storing fear memories and found that actions of a brain chemical called CREB (cyclic adenosine monophosphate response element-binding protein) are key to memory. The research seems to confirm the roles of both CREB and that section of the lateral amygdala in making fear memories.

And at SUNY Downstate in Brooklyn, neuroscientists have erased fear memories in mice by delivering an experimental drug directly into their brains (ouch!) to block a substance called PKMzeta, which is known to be involved in strengthening permanent memory networks among neurons.

The Toll of Mental Illness—and Anxiety

Everyday anxiety causes a great deal of damage but doesn't get the research attention of other serious mental illnesses, says Joseph LeDoux, a pioneer in the study of the biological basis of emotions, especially fear.

Anxiety disorders affect about 18 percent of the adult population (more than 20 million people). By contrast, bipolar disorder (5.7 million), schizophrenia (2.4 million), and major depressive disorder

(14.8 million) total fewer than 23 million—about 21 percent, combined.

More than half of mental health visits in the United States every year are for anxiety or related conditions, including PTSD, generalized anxiety disorder, obsessive-compulsive disorder, schizophrenia, and depression. Most often anxiety either drives these conditions or makes them unbearable.

"But even people not pathologically anxious are troubled. It's insidious: Fear is immediate; but anxiety is about what may or may not happen," said LeDoux. "It's a consequence of having the normal mechanisms of fear in a brain that can also think in elaborate ways," he said. "There's a joke: If you aren't anxious about this, something else will come along."

In fact, our brains are wired for alertness, which can translate into anxiety, he said, with more connections running from the trigger-happy flight or fight amygdala to the thinking neocortex than the other way around: "This may explain why, once an emotion is aroused, it is so hard for us to turn it off at will."

Memory plays a key role in fear, anxiety, and identity. "We are our memories," he said. "One of the big mysteries is how memory makes us who we are. Hopefully, we'll understand it better soon, and come to terms with how memory is potentiated in the brain, and how it is processed in different systems. We don't understand yet how those systems interact."

LeDoux and others are investigating reconsolidation—the period during which memories are vulnerable to change or even erasure. Strengthening the synapses—the junctions between neurons that hold long-term memories—requires protein synthesis. LeDoux and other researchers have recently found that if this process is disrupted while a long-standing memory is being recalled, the memory can actually be made fleeting.

Meanwhile, LeDoux has a practical biologically based suggestion for better mental health and less anxiety: "In general we need to be more proactive about mental health, beginning with young children. One of the best things we can do with kids from kindergarten on up is to show them breathing exercises. These engage the parasympathetic nervous system; this slows things down, relieves anxiety, and helps with focus. It's the same idea as with yoga and meditation. Breathing helps restrain neurons that control fight-flight response. It's all about calming down the body and the brain. We know kids need to have their bodies eat the right things. We can also help them learn to master emotions."

What's Next? And What About My Brain?

It will be awhile before researchers are using memory medication or injections for either remembering or forgetting on your brain. Nevertheless, they're making significant progress, especially in understating the basics of memory and learning. The coming epidemic of Alzheimer's disease has been a potent incentive, and pharmaceutical companies, academic centers, and the government are investing billions of dollars in research.

One route to improving memory lies in the relatively new field of epigenetics: the study of changes in DNA that don't affect the genetic code but do influence gene expression—that is, how actively a gene is used to make protein. Within decades, some research suggests, fiddling around with gene expression might lead to reversing or resolving a slew of memory and learning disorders from Alzheimer's disease to mental retardation.

Flipping a chemical switch to turn a specific gene on or off, it turns out, can have a profound impact on long-term memory. That switch can be a drug or even a change in the environment that acts as a kind of volume control for gene expression.

Gene expression is critical to memory formation. As a person learns and a memory takes shape, the ebbs and flows in the activity of neurons provoke synthesis of new proteins, which help to cement or create connections between nerve cells. In this process, genes are first transcribed into RNA (ribonucleic acid), which is then translated into protein.

Over the past few years, scientists have learned more about the chemicals in making memories through epigenetics. The process requires activity from enzymes called histone acetyltransferases (HATs). These HATs attach chemical units called acetyl groups to histones, which then open up the DNA and allow some changes in gene expression. They do this by counteracting their enzyme opposites: the histone deacetylases (HDACs), which remove the acetyl groups from histones and close up DNA.

Researchers tested this in a group of mice by first blacking out their memories of a fearful place and then injecting some of the mice daily for four weeks with a chemical that blocks the HDACs. This allowed the HATs to unwrap DNA from its protein packaging and make changes in gene expression, with the result that the memories of the treated mice were restored.

Further experiments with animals suggest that retrieving lost memories might be possible even after severe brain damage, and that epigenetic mechanisms are central to this recovery. Even more provocative, if medicine can revive memory after brain damage, could it also correct genetic brain problems such as mental retardation? Maybe.

Working with mice that were born with a genetic disorder that resembled mental retardation, scientists found that if the mice received an HDAC inhibitor three hours before a training session, they didn't seem to have learning problems. This work suggests that even ingrained mental lacks might be able to be fixed through epigenetic manipulation.

Erasing memories doesn't have to involve pharmacology. Researchers at New York University and the University of Texas used behavioral modification therapy rather than drugs to weaken fear memories: extinction training, in which the known fear stimulus is repeated again and again until there is no reaction; and reconsolidation blockage, in which fear memories are blocked as they are being recalled (reconsolidated) and thus in a stage vulnerable to change. By applying the extinction therapy during that labile reconsolidation window, researchers were able to disrupt fear memories in mice without drugs.

And an MIT group came up with a drug-free way to restore mouse memories: changing the rodents' environment. Enriching the surroundings—giving the mice new toys to play with and running wheels that enabled them to exercise—also increased the number of acetyl groups on histones, apparently revving up the expression of memory genes, just as the HDAC inhibitors did. That finding may help explain why scholars and academics, who presumably live in an intellectually enriched world, are less susceptible to Alzheimer's disease. A mentally stimulating job could be another form of environmental enrichment for humans. It's all even more evidence for staying mentally active and involved in challenging brain work and play.

Although epigenetic alteration hasn't been done deliberately in humans (yet), the work shows tremendous potential to mold memories and, in the future, reverse cognitive disorders ranging from Alzheimer's disease to mental retardation. Scientists also suggest that in the future, we may be implanting microchips or processors directly into the brain to increase memory storage space.

Meanwhile, researchers are nowhere near being able to selectively erase memory in humans. In fact, the very thought brings up many practical and ethical issues. For example, we have to be very certain about which memories to erase and what the repercussions could be. Perhaps a domino-like effect would crash other memories connected to the forgotten ones or could interfere with learning in the present and future. What if erasing bad memories disrupts good ones? And what about brainwashing by government agents? There's always the danger some people will use science for personal gain, for political power, or even to impose what they believe are good values on others. That won't change. But by the time scientists are able to rub out memories effectively, we'll no doubt have some of these other issues resolved.

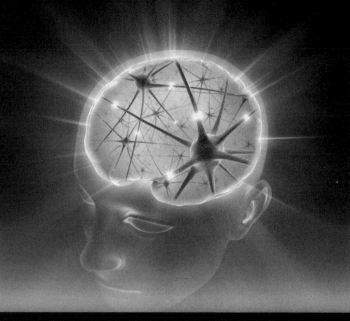

CHAPTER FOUR

Digital You

What the Digital Explosion Is Doing to Your iBrain

IN BRIEF

Forget book learning, physical classrooms, and didactic teaching, even physical books themselves. Brains today learn through Internet interaction, wirelessly at lightning speed and all the time, networked globally across social, political, and geographical boundaries. Scientists aren't sure exactly what that's really doing to our brains, but they're sure it's doing something, and that microprocessors that will WiFi our brains directly to the Internet are next up.

Then: The World Wide Web was an obscure technology used mainly by academics, the military, and some ambitious news reporters. Portable phones were the size of lunch boxes; rare; and limited in scope, just like landline phones, rabbit-ear TVs, books, and classrooms.

NOW: Everybody's digitalized every way through a clutch of ever-smaller instruments and implements, and cell phones rule: 85 percent of adult Americans have cell phones.

Tomorrow: Implanted digital contraptions on direct-dial to your brain will replace your external electronics and allow for an incessant stream of endless information. Next step: your bionic brain.

Are You Born Digital—or a Digital Immigrant?

It's Saturday morning, and your WiFi connection is down, and you can't find your smartphone. You have no access to phone numbers, addresses, datebook, e-mail, family photos, blog, Facebook, MySpace, bank accounts, text messages—or no way of settling an argument about where the Danube meets the sea.

Do you panic? It depends. Are you a digital native—born digital into a world where computers, the Internet, cell phones, handheld smartphones, and other digital technology have always been in your life, and where there never was a time without them? Or are you a digital immigrant—someone born before 1980 who has had to assimilate new technology, because it's all new and pretty strange to you?

Consider John McCain, who admitted during the 2008 election that he doesn't or can't use the Internet, versus President Barack Obama, whose BlackBerry seemed grafted to his hand. More than years separate them: it's a neurotechnological shift in worldview that is reflected in their attitudes, their actions, and their brains.

The terms *digital native* and *digital immigrant* were coined in an article in 2001 by Marc Prensky, a developer of games, who says learning has radically changed because of computers and the Internet.

No doubt, living in a digital world has changed the way we work, live, and interact, with e-mail and incessant texting replacing letters and even phone calls, and how we acquire, use, and dispense information. A majority of us are hooked up to a PDA, MP3, cell phone, iPhone, smartphone, iPod, BlackBerry, Twitter, Facebook, MySpace, and LinkedIn, and walking around with a WiFi apparatus stuck in one ear and an iPod in the other. In fact, do you own a phonebook? A dictionary? A library card? A landline? Thought not. Some public schools are even doing away with some paper textbooks in favor of open source, and free, digital versions or online learning. There's even a mindfulness meditation application for your iPhone.

There've been many observations about the impact of this digital world on how we think (and on how we spell, but that's another issue). Extensive time spent online must be changing the way the brain processes information, so it must also be changing the physical brain.

But that should come as no surprise: Extensive time spent shopping, playing poker, or indulging in addictive substances also changes your brain. Research has been showing for decades that how we use mind and body changes our brain and brain activity. Hours spent with today's digital technology and on the Internet are bound to result in a shift in neural processing. So far, though, no one knows exactly how. Most clinical studies have looked only at the impact of video games.

The Brains of Digital Natives

Although there are few studies as yet of the brains of digital natives in action, observations of digital activity have found the following:

- *Greater connectivity.* A digital native lives in cyberspace, more a resident of the network than of a geographical location. The Internet crosses national and cultural borders, and its users are connected almost around the clock.

- *More interactive learning.* Digital natives aren't passive users of the Internet. According to a recent study by the Pew Internet and American Life Project, more than 50 percent of today's teenagers have created digital media.
- *Heightened visual senses.* Research shows that interacting with video games improves peripheral vision and shortens reaction time to visual stimuli.
- *Faster neural shifting.* This occurs between images, ideas, and onscreen resources.
- *Shorthand communication.* Abbreviated wording produces compact messages more like those of a poet than a novelist.

Today's digital natives tend to absorb information quickly in small bites (bytes); have a short attention span; and multitask obsessively, paying partial attention to many things. They are able to block out background noise and distractions (TV, video, and your voice) when they need to focus and are accustomed to finding what they need to know in cyberspace, not in books. Startlingly, some high-achieving university students have said—without a trace of chagrin—that they don't read books. It's all on the Internet.

Academics are on it. An interdisciplinary collaboration called Digital Natives that both supports and studies young people in a digital age is being run out of Harvard's Berkman Center for Internet and Society and the Research Center for Information Law at the University of St. Gallen in Switzerland. Codirectors John Palfrey of Harvard and Urs Gasser at St. Gallen are also authors of a book, *Born Digital: Understanding the First Generation of Digital Natives,* that looks at the promises and pitfalls of today's wired culture: issues of privacy; information overload; information accuracy; cyberstalking; and, optimistically, greater global connectivity.

Palfrey and Gasser say there's cause for optimism. Although some older folks fear our kids' (and grandkids') brains are interacting less with others, they may actually be interacting more, and all the time, with one another, with machines, and with the whole world. They are networked not just at home and school but globally through international contacts, special interests, communities, and social networks.

Their worlds (and brains) are interactive—that is, information goes both ways—so they aren't traditional students, learning passively from one-way lectures. Residents of developing nations are drawn into the network as never before. In India, the poor may not have running water at home, but they use cell phones to text message. In 2009, Facebook launched a Swahili version.

The Bad, the Good, and the Unknown Effects of Technology

In spite of all this connectivity, some researchers say social skills might be suffering. In *iBrain: Surviving the Technological Alteration of the Modern Mind*, coauthors Gary Small and Gigi Vorgan say the new technology may be sharpening some thinking skills but undermining others, and long-term attention isn't the only casualty. Worsening are face-to-face social skills, such as reading facial expressions during conversation or grasping the emotional context of a subtle gesture. Small, a professor at the Semel Institute for Neuroscience and Human Behavior at UCLA, cites a 2002 Stanford University study that found that for every hour we spend on our computers, traditional face-to-face interaction time with other people drops by nearly thirty minutes.

There are some other concerns about how those brains are being used. Digital natives tend to take in huge amounts of information and hyperlink ideas, spinning off one idea onto another, and they are obsessed with near-instant communication. In fact, the mental data processing of digital natives sounds quite a lot like a condition some of us digital immigrants have, but we call it ADHD. And indeed, immersion in the digital world has been accused of contributing to the rise in ADHD. Experts say children, in particular, who spend extensive time with TV, video, and computers are at a much higher risk of developing attention disorders. But it could be we need a touch of this to function today.

However, all such discussions are based mostly on observation, opinion and hot debates over articles such as the 2008 *Atlantic Monthly* piece "Is Google Making Us Stupid?" (yes, says author Nicolas Carr; maybe not, say others), and similar articles along the lines of "Is the Internet Warping Our Brains?"

It's correct to keep posing these questions. We really don't know what the hyped world of cybercommunication and information is doing to our brains because we don't know enough yet about how our brains work. So far, few studies have actually compared the brains of digital users and nonusers in action, possibly because it's difficult to find a large sample group that isn't Internet savvy.

Small and his colleagues did two of these few studies. They put twelve digital natives and twelve digital newbies (ages fifty-five to seventy-six) into an fMRI scanner and watched brain activity as they read or surfed the Net. When reading text, both groups showed the same type of brain activity. But when doing an Internet search, the digital natives showed significant increases in activity in parts of the brain controlling decision making and complex reasoning (the frontal pole, anterior temporal region, anterior and posterior cingulate, and hippocampus), whereas the brains of the digital newbies reacted about the same as to text.

Following up with an additional study with the same groups, the study team found it took only seven days of Internet practice at about one hour per day for a newbie's brain to show the same increased neural network activation as in the digital natives, and also activity in the middle frontal gyrus and inferior frontal gyrus—areas of the brain known to be important in working memory and decision making.

Although these findings are preliminary and based on a very small sample, Small says they suggest Internet use has physiological effects and could have potential benefits for aging brains, improving brain circuitry and boosting cognition in older adults. Research is continuing, with studies looking further for both positive and negative brain effects from Internet use.

Meanwhile, a 2009 Dutch study that compared actual cognitive performance before and after Internet immersion showed the end

HOW CELL PHONES AFFECT YOUR IBRAIN

Exposure to the electrical currents that drive digital toys, at least those from cell phones, may affect the brain in a not-so-productive way. One study showed cell phone use at bedtime may promote insomnia: people exposed to cell phone signals in talk mode took nearly twice as long to fall asleep. Another study put people to sleep with cell phones strapped to their heads and found that when the phones were switched on at random, those brains responded with a peak in alpha brain waves associated with alertness—perhaps an effort by the brain to overcome electrical interference from the phones. But scientists predict they may resolve that in the next few decades: a computer chip in your brain will replace that external cell phone.

result in performance may not be much different. The researchers took 191 healthy elders (ages sixty-four to seventy-five), gave them a year of varying levels of computer training and exposure, and compared them to 45 elders with no interest in computers. Standard tests of cognitive functions at four and twelve months showed no differences between the two groups.

The Future Is Closer Than You Think

Written in 2006, the science-fiction novel *Rainbows End* projects massive innovations along current lines of research in barely two decades. Author Vernor Vinge postulates a world in 2025 where digital technology has almost everything and everyone WiFied and networked, and Alzheimer's disease is not only curable but reversible.

The main character, renowned seventy-five-year-old Chinese-American poet Robert Gu, has been out of commission for years with Alzheimer's disease. Thanks to advances in medicine, he has recovered enough to reenter the world. But Robert, who had barely used e-mail before his illness, finds himself desperately out of touch.

Laptops are way obsolete, and even handhelds are gone: people "wear" computers, special contact lenses, and sensors that show multiple layers of reality and communication, as well as sensors that can locate them and show their locations in blueprint-like detail. Anyone can silent-message instantly and also project a virtual (and seemingly real) identity and background: say, that of a talking unicorn in a medieval landscape.

Those predictions may be too conservative, according to other future thinkers. A brain implant to access the Internet is on its way soon, they say—either as a true implant or in a helmet with sensors to pick up both WiFi signals and brain activity. The Institute for the Future says in its 2009 ten-year forecast that physical and digital realities will soon be "seamlessly integrated," adding new layers of reality to our brains and our senses and even remaking our basic concepts of self. Most digital natives already have multiple virtual versions of their "selves."

Futurist Ray Kurzweil predicts we will have true artificial intelligence in a few decades and a merging of mind and computer by midcentury, with our brains able to be downloaded into silicon so our consciousness can live on forever, perhaps even downloaded into robots—or into an avatar, an ageless biological clone.

Johnny Mnemonic

In this film, based on a 1981 short story by William Gibson, Johnny Mnemonic (Keanu Reeves) is a data trafficker in the future with a brain implant that can hold 160 GB of sensitive data (a huge amount in 1995, when the film was made). But a data run goes bad when he uploads a valuable "package" that both exceeds his implant's safety level and sets assassins after him to retrieve the information.

Uses of the Digital You

There is a phenomenal interest in a cybermemory from the tens of millions with Alzheimer's disease already or those at risk in the near future—and from the military. The U.S. Defense Advanced Research Projects Agency (DARPA) has a keen interest. It has invested millions of dollars developing such personal digital technology, including LifeLog, a program that would track and collect in searchable format all of an individual's "transactional data," such as what we buy and who gets our e-mail.

The potential use of all this personal data is awesome and might make some of us a bit queasy. It allows for jacking into our most basic (and heretofore considered private) information, without giving us much control over how it's used.

There's a major limitation that neuroscience is unlikely to overcome soon: so far, the digital collections can't capture actual thoughts or emotions needed to make sense of all of these memories—at least not yet.

There's also no effective way to indicate the relative importance of each digital bit as it's recorded—to show, for example, that information about your retirement fund is more important than an e-mail about your dental appointment ten years ago. Your brain would need a librarian with knowledge of the importance, emotions, and thoughts behind these digital memos to put them in context. Oh. You already have one. It's your mind.

Brainstorm

A team of scientists in this 1983 movie invent a brain-reading device that can record sensations directly from a person's brain. The device can be played back and even sent to a telephone headset so anyone can experience all the sensations of the original wearer. The possibilities to virtually experience theme park adventures, sex, and even death raise issues and complications, along with (of course) military ambitions for torture or brainwashing.

What About My Body? Balancing the iBrain and Your Sensory Self

We've become so committed to digital and neurological technology to enhance the brain that we might forget the brain is part of the body. Although the digital world has many benefits, it also tends to isolate us and our children from physical interaction and from the physical world around us: the world of socializing, touch, texture, color, movement, taste, and scent. Research is showing that face-to-face is still best for much learning.

Apparently the brains of babies and children need other people, especially parents and other caregivers, to learn. Social connection and interaction, scientists are finding, are important to early learning. Children take in more information by looking at another person face-to-face than by looking at a person on a big plasma TV screen. Children also learn what's important in their environment by watching where a grown-up's gaze goes, which helps them figure out what's worth paying attention to.

A lack of human connection and interactivity may have a potent impact on the brains of young children who sit for hours in front of a television or computer game that may overstimulate sight and hearing senses but neglect other channels of perception. Children who are chronically exposed to TV, videos, and the Internet don't develop a well-balanced sensory palette and are at higher risk for developing attention deficit hyperactivity disorder instead. In fact, the American Academy of Pediatrics recommends no television or video viewing for children under the age of two years.

And it doesn't hurt adults any to increase sensory experience. We could take some tips from sensory integration therapy, recommended for children who have difficulties or imbalances in the way their brains handle input from the senses. The exercises for kids can be translated to sedentary adults as well.

Try taking a break from the computer to turn on and tune up the other senses. Tactile sensations awaken with clay and fingerpaints— or kneading bread, digging in the garden, knitting, wiggling your toes in the sand, or painting a piece of furniture. Vestibular movement, or balance, is enhanced by jumping, dancing, Tai Chi, yoga, and other whole body activities. Aromatherapy (gardening and cooking again) awakens the nose. Expand vision with lava lamps, distant seeing, and games of catch and throw, and excite hearing with the sounds of bubbling fountains and by making acoustic music.

HOW TO TELL WHEN YOUR BRAIN HAS A DIGITAL SOCIAL ADDICTION

As if you needed to be told: An addiction to poking, pinging, tweeting, texting, IM-ing, and e-mailing seems to be an issue for many of us. Some research suggests it sets off the dopamine reward circuit, the same as other addictions.

There are dozens of Internet links referring to it. Here's a list compiled from various sources on determining if you have a digital social networking addiction:

- You lose sleep keeping up with e-mail and social networks. E-mail's the first thing you check in the morning and the last at night. In fact, you never log out.
- You spend more than three hours a day trolling, obsessed with checking to see who's writing to or about you. How many "results" do you have on Google? How many Facebook "friends"? How many hits on your blog?
- A lost Internet connection, cell phone dead zone, or computer crash puts you in a panic.
- Internet social networks are your main way of connecting with others. You have more than one such account. In fact, you have more friends on MySpace or Facebook than you do in real life. In fact, what is real life?
- You procrastinate and ignore work in favor of Facebook, Twitter, MySpace, e-mail. The list goes on—but your work does not.

Beyond Digital: The Serious Need for Play

Psychologists and a battery of studies say childhood play is crucial for social, emotional, and cognitive development, and it's pretty important for adult brains as well. In fact, studies show that children and animals that do not play when they are young may have behavioral difficulties later. These experts aren't talking about computer or video games or even sports but something they call free play: imaginative and rambunctious fooling around that involves moving—jumping, running, wrestling—and aimless and creative actions.

Boston College developmental psychologist Peter Gray theorizes that play developed early on in human history to foster cooperation and sharing and to counteract aggression and selfishness. But there isn't much free play today. Concerned about getting kids into the right kindergarten as well as college (or protecting them from the dangers of the streets), parents are sacrificing playtime for more structured and indoor activities. As early as preschool, youngsters' after-school hours are now being filled with music lessons and sports and, not much later, with digital games, texting, and the Internet. All of this takes away imaginative and rambunctious cavorting and face-to-face contact that foster creativity and cooperation.

The positive effect of play is important for adults too. It helps prevent burnout and gives your brain a break from head work. Work will always get done, and the happiness and renewed energy you experience from playing will more than compensate for the time lost. Gray even suggests the recent economic collapse might be connected to some extent to the greed and selfishness of adults who don't know how to play.

Experts suggest you treat your inner child to some free-form sensory integration therapy:

- *Body play.* Participate in some form of active movement that has no time pressures or expected outcome. (If you are exercising just to burn fat, that is *not* play.)

- *Object play.* Use your hands to create something you enjoy. It can be anything from a sand castle to a watercolor painting. There doesn't have to be a specific goal.
- *Social play.* Join other people in seemingly purposeless social activities, from small talk to verbal jousting.

If you are still not sure what to try, remember what you enjoyed doing as a child, and translate those memories into activities that fit your life today. You might even spark your memory better if you spend a little time around kids—and get them off the Internet as well.

What's Next? And What About My Brain?

If you're reading this book, you're probably an Internet user and already have a digital avatar (or two) and a digital memory of sorts. One of the paramount reasons we love our computers so is the way they store memories for us, from photos to e-mails and agendas.

Sometimes we crave an infallible memory—a repository for all we have said, seen, read, heard, and done—that we could access as needed. We could use, in fact, a digital brain. Gordon Bell has one, or an approximation of one: he has a digital record of his life and sometimes refers to it as his surrogate brain. Since 1998, the Microsoft research scientist has been recording just about his entire life. All the documents and artifacts from his personal life and his long career in the computer business are in digital form in a Microsoft project called MyLifeBits.

The concept actually predates computers. It was proposed at the end of World War II by presidential science advisor Vannevar Bush, who craved a memory extender that he called a memex—back then, that would have been a microfilm-based device to record and store all communications.

With today's technology, that's a staggering amount of information. The system records Bell's telephone calls, programs playing on radio and television, a copy of every e-mail, every Web page he visits and file he opens, and a transcript of every instant message he sends or receives. When Bell is on the go, MyLifeBits continually uploads his location and environs from a portable global positioning system device and a camera worn around his neck activated by motion detectors.

And why not? We've got the digital storage capacity, and it's cheap. Today, a hard drive can hold a terabyte (1 trillion bytes) of data, enough to store everything you read (e-mails, Web pages, papers, and books), all the music you purchase, eight hours of speech, and ten pictures a day for the next sixty years. Within a decade, you will be able to carry the same amount of information in your cell phone's flash memory, while connecting wirelessly to an inexpensive 4-terabyte drive on your PC. In twenty years, a few hundred dollars will buy 250 terabytes of storage—enough to satisfy anyone's recording needs for more than one hundred years.

You already do some form of this today with off-the-shelf technology. As hardware and software for digital storage have improved, more and more of us have electronic chronicles of our lives—digital photographs, letters, memos, agendas, and address lists—on our hard drives.

Some of this is just plain trivia, like photos of those who passed Bell on a street in San Francisco in 2007, recorded automatically and forever by his motion-triggered digital camera. Some cynics refer to it as MyLifeBlob or cybernarcissism. But it has valuable potential uses. For example, sensors could monitor your bodily functions 24/7, creating a pattern of normality and alerting you or your doctors to a variation that could predict an illness, such as a potential heart attack or stroke. Health records, including digital x-rays, can be stored on your cell phone. In fact, some of us don't have to wait: in 2009, giant health maintenance organization Kaiser Permanente began offering its northern California members a free flash drive with the basics: the member's emergency contacts, physicians, medical issues, allergies, current medications, and lab results for the past year.

By the century's end (or sooner according to Ray Kurzweil), you might have all this on a backup chip implanted in your brain. Seriously. In the not-very-far future, neuroscientists predict, we will

HAPPINESS IS CONTAGIOUS—IF YOU'RE NEARBY

Want to live a happier life? Try surrounding yourself with happy friends or at least find friends with happy friends. A study in the *British Medical Journal* says happiness can quickly go viral within your physically close social network.

Researchers looked at twenty years' worth of data on more than five thousand individuals and found that when any one person was happy, his or her friends became more likely to share that joy. Benefits spread out to three degrees of separation, meaning a better chance at happiness for not only their friends' friends but also their friends' friends' friends.

But don't go thinking your ten thousand buddies on Facebook will bring you happiness, because your happy friends need to be physically in your space. The researchers found that the strength of the effect dissipates over physical distance, with next-door neighbors and friends living nearby getting the biggest boost. Surprisingly, sadness made very little headway within social networks, paling in comparison to the communal effects of happiness.

have computer chips in our brains to expand memory (or beef up brain areas lost to Alzheimer's disease) or hold information. Indeed, brain-machine interfaces are part of the technology already, and biological clones to host your consciousness are a possibility in the far future (see "Your Bionic Brain," p. 101).

CHAPTER FIVE

Looking Inside Your Brain
The Magic of Neuroimaging

IN BRIEF

For thousands of years, healers yearned in vain to see inside a living, thinking brain without opening the skull. But until recently, the technology has given only tantalizing glimpses. The new brain imaging, made possible by functional MRI (fMRI) scans, changed all that, taking scientists inside the workings of the living human brain in action and in real time. Rapidly accelerating technology promises even more and better tools for viewing, diagnosing, repairing, and perhaps even improving your brain in the near future—tools that even exceed those of science fiction.

Then: Phrenology, the pseudoscience of mapping brain function by skull shape, gave way to actual brain images from X-rays and external electrodes. These gave glimpses of the brain's geography and some neural activity and were able to show when something was seriously amiss.

Now: Sophisticated neural imaging allows us to see inside the brain in greater detail than ever before possible to aid in diagnosis and brain surgery—and, some say, to map, record, and predict some of our emotions and actions, such as lying and a predilection for violence.

Tomorrow: Better knowledge of brain function will allow scientists to interpret brain scans more precisely. And neuroimaging will jump into another dimension, literally, with three-dimensional videos and perhaps microscopic nanobots that noninvasively swim into the brain to record neural activity in detail and treat everything from mental illness to stroke.

Although we take brain scans for granted today, they are in fact near magical. Scientists are able to look inside a living, working, thinking, feeling human brain without cracking the skull. And it has happened in record time. The technology has galloped from X-rays to electroencephalography to electronic scans in barely more than a century.

Many mysteries are being revealed this way. With this new tool, scientists add to our basic knowledge of normal brain activities, brain dysfunction, and brain disease. They are rapidly mapping the geography, topography, wiring, and biochemistry of your most vital organ and figuring out where and how to intervene when there's a problem.

Without neuroimaging, brain surgery would be, as it was in the not-very-distant past, more of a blind search. We would not know ahead of time what sections are involved in trauma or tumors, or where to put electrodes to stop tremors, or even where in the brain some seizures begin. Imaging has revealed abnormalities of activity, size, or networks in the brains of autistic children and people with Alzheimer's disease, multiple sclerosis, schizophrenia, and other conditions. Now we can predict when and perhaps where some hidden illnesses, from Alzheimer's disease to stroke, are hovering. This technology is a truly remarkable achievement that saves or betters thousands of lives every year and promises to offer information about the detailed workings of the brain in the very near future.

The fMRI, which registers blood flow in a living, and maybe lying, brain, raised the bar on what we can know and see about brains in action. We can watch and record the brainstorm of an epileptic convulsion, the progress of a blood clot in a stroke, and where and how in your brain a flash of feeling sends a flush of blood.

It seems there's an announcement almost weekly related to brain scans, and many of them are about the controversial findings of the so-called mind-reading aspects of the fMRI: that fMRI images have mapped sections for specific thoughts or feelings and can tell where and when someone is thinking what. That has led to some heated discussions about what it's truly possible to know about the mind through today's technology, and what such knowledge might mean in law enforcement, employment, and social relationships.

TOOLS FOR LOOKING INSIDE THE BRAIN

Today's array of sophisticated technologies astounds. Here's a review of how they developed over time, how they work, and what that alphabet soup of acronyms means.

X-ray. Discovered in 1895. Electromagnetic radiation passes through an object where differing densities absorb it at different levels, creating a negative image on light-sensitive film. It's also called Röntgen radiation after Wilhelm Conrad Röntgen, who was awarded the first Nobel Prize for its discovery. A new form, digital X-ray, uses less radiation and can be viewed immediately.

EEG (electroencephalograph). Provides a direct reading of the brain's electrical activity, taken from multiple electrodes placed on the scalp and displayed as squiggly lines on a chart. It's been in use since the 1920s and is relatively inexpensive and effective. But it can't detect activity deep inside the brain very well or produce an image.

CAT (computed axial tomography; also CT, computed tomography). Uses special X-ray equipment and computers to create cross-sectional pictures of the body at different angles (*tomography* means "imaging by sections"). It's been used since the 1970s and has the advantage over X-rays of being able to show body sections behind other parts and in much more detail.

PET (positron emission tomography). A small amount of radioactive material is given to the patient and then detected by special cameras in images that allow researchers to observe and measure activity in different parts of the brain by monitoring blood flow and other substances such as oxygen and glucose.

MRI (magnetic resonance imaging). Magnetic fields are used to generate a computer image of internal structures in the body. MRI is particularly good for imaging the brain and soft tissues.

fMRI (functional magnetic resonance imaging). This brain scan can measure blood flow and other activity in the brain in action and in real time.

MEG (magnetoencephalography). Measures the magnetic fields created by the electric current flowing within the neurons and detects brain activity associated with various functions in real time.

SPECT (single photon emission computed tomography). Uses a small amount of radioactive tracer in a way similar to a PET to measure and monitor blood flow in the brain and produce a three-dimensional image.

DTI (diffusion tensor imaging). Measures the flow of water molecules along the white matter, or myelin, which makes up 50 percent of the brain and connects many regions. The technology is not yet easily interpreted.

Smile, Say Cheese? Not Exactly: How an MRI Works

The MRI and fMRI are the most popular brain scan technologies today, especially when researchers want to see a brain in action. Volunteers from meditating monks to copulating couples have added to our knowledge by being imaged in action with an MRI.

Here is what the MRI machine is, and what it's really doing while you think (or busy yourself). The scanner weighs around 12 tons and costs about $2.5 million. It's a large electromagnetic cylinder constructed from superconducting wire cooled by helium that generates powerful magnetic fields. The levels of these fields are twenty-five thousand to eighty thousand times the strength of the earth's magnetic field. They are so powerful that people must remove all metal items before entering the shielded area. Flying metal objects pulled by an MRI machine have killed people.

Patients with pacemakers or metal implants can't even go into the room, which itself is heavily fortified with steel and uses sound-proofing technologies to muffle the bone-shaking noise produced when the magnets work their magic.

People being scanned are slid into the long, narrow cylindrical magnet, which creates a magnetic field around the head. It's important to remain still, so the head is usually placed in a restraint with foam wedges inside the head coil (nicknamed "the cage") to reduce head motion, which can blur the images. Sometimes a bite-bar—a custom-made mouthpiece attached to the head rest—is used to help keep the head still. Images are taken every one or two seconds, the MRI producing up to thousands of images in each scanning session, and it's very loud. The noise, described as a loud, constant, rapid hammering, may be muffled somewhat by earphones or a headset. It continues for fifteen minutes to an hour or more depending on the diagnosis or the study.

Radio waves are sent through the magnetic field. Sensors read the signals, and a computer uses the information to construct an image, which can show both surface and deep brain structures with a high degree of anatomical detail and detect minute changes in these structures. The fMRI images created are based on magnetic signals and blood flow in the brain. When neurons are active, they consume more oxygen, which is pulled out of the hemoglobin in red blood cells from nearby capillaries; the brain responds to this increased need for oxygen by sending out more—and for reasons that are not yet fully understood, it actually sends a greater amount than is needed. There is a delay of about five seconds between neural activity and blood flow change, which leads to differences in the relative concentration of oxygenated hemoglobin in those active brain areas. Because the iron in hemoglobin is magnetically sensitive, there are measurable magnetic differences between blood cells with and those without oxygen. The MRI scanner measures and notes these differences and produces an image.

Picture This: Psychopath, Pedophile, Autistic Toddler

Scientists are finding many anomalies in the brains of some groups that could help with diagnosis, treatment, or—some fear—preemptive identification and incarceration of those whose brains show potential for crime. For example:

- A preliminary finding shows that the brains of nine men who were diagnosed as psychopaths are different from most other people's. Using a new scanning technique called DTI-MRI, the team at the Institute of Psychiatry at King's College, London, found that a white-matter tract called the uncinate fasciculus, which connects the amygdala and the orbitofrontal cortex, differed significantly between the psychopaths and the control group: the more extreme the psychopathy, the greater the abnormality. Some of the psychopaths in the study had committed multiple rapes, manslaughter, and attempted murder. (Incidentally, none of the men were incarcerated at the time of the study.) And pedophiles, it seems, have less white matter connecting the brain regions involved in sexual arousal.

- Researchers at the University of Bonn in Germany have found through DTI scanning that the more some people seek new experiences, the stronger their connections are from the hippocampus and amygdala (brain regions involved in decision making and emotion) to the ventral and mesial striatum areas, which process information related to emotion and reward. The scientists also found that the subjects who were most dependent on social approval had stronger-than-normal connections between the striatum and the prefrontal cortex, a brain area involved in higher-order decision making.

- Researchers looking at autistic children found a correlation between the size of the brain's sentry center, the amygdala, and behavior. The amygdala was larger in two- and four-year-old children with autism.

These are just some of the brains in which scientists are finding identifiable anomalies, according to recent studies. But scientists still are left with a puzzle: although they are collecting information that will be valuable eventually, right now they don't know exactly what these findings mean.

Scanning the Other Half of Your Brain: Why White Matter Matters

A powerful new kind of MRI is confirming the importance of the white matter, or myelin, that makes up 50 percent of the brain—what neuroscientist R. Douglas Fields refers to in the title of his new book as *The Other Brain*.

Although we often refer to our brain as "gray matter," about half the human brain is white matter, a larger fraction than in any other animal (a rat's brain, for example, is only 10 percent white matter). The gray matter in the thin layer that is the cortex is indeed involved in so-called higher processing, but the rest of your brain is also busy, said Fields, who is chief of the nervous system development and plasticity section at the National Institutes of Health and founding editor-in-chief of *Neuron Glia Biology*, a scientific journal.

Fields started out studying how the brain develops, which led to neuroplasticity and memory, and then to epigenetics, and that led to glial cells and how they work—and that made him realize how little we know about the brain.

"We know as much about the brain as Darwin knew about molecular biology. We have great new techniques, but still very very rudimentary knowledge," said Fields. "The foundations of our ideas in neuroscience have not changed in one hundred years. They are all based on synapses, and all of our remedies for treating psychiatric illness are about regulating neurotransmitters."

"Yet synapses use only twenty-five nanometers of space in the brain—an area so small that it can be seen only by an electron microscope. Studying synapses is like studying transistors—the elemental unit of change or information switching in the brain—but after transistors, you've got integrated circuits. We need to look at how the brain works together, not in sections."

For some time, neuroscientists—erroneously—dismissed white matter as mere insulation. It is indeed insulation of sorts, but now we know it is much more. To be precise, white matter is the area of the brain comprising millions of axons that connect brain cells in circuits. Myelin is the membrane wrapped around axons like electrical tape to insulate them and makes up the brain's "data lines" carrying information between neurons in distant areas of the brain. It looks white, says Fields, because it is high in fat.

White matter turns out to be the glue that connects many disparate parts of your brain, crucial to communication among brain cells— in particular, how speedily and efficiently impulses race along the pathways in the thinking, sensory, and motor processing regions of your brain.

DTI, one of the newer imaging techniques, is confirming the vital role of white matter to brain health. Malfunctioning or damaged white matter is involved in multiple sclerosis, Alzheimer's disease, epilepsy, and perhaps mental illness.

Several kinds of glial cells make up white matter and hold many secrets to the brain that we've barely begun to explore, says Fields. DTI imaging is giving new insights into these networks, leading to a better understanding of how the brain works and, perhaps more important, helping discover why disconnections between parts of the brain might contribute to mental illnesses such as schizophrenia, autism, and drug abuse. DTI is still a work in progress: it maps white matter tracts by measuring water diffusion along nerve fibers and is not yet easy to interpret.

Meanwhile, "We do know our brain circuits are being molded and refined according to the environment. We develop the brain we need," said Fields. Knowing more about how the brain is molded by the environment will help us know more about how the brain works and how it ages.

"We'll know a lot more in the next decade, but I think we need to look ahead fifty years, when we can really understand how the human brain operates."

The Limits of Brain Scans

Brain scans are of enormous benefit and represent a huge advance in diagnosis and treatment. And they are of keen interest to us as potential patients with brain disorders and injuries. With all the vivid colors and scientific wording, it seems to most of us that the sophisticated images are also an accurate sign of brain activity.

But hold on: this tool can also be co-opted for law and commerce or, some say, a circus act. Brain scan news increasingly focuses on what MRIs purport to reveal about emotions, thoughts, and propensities: that by looking at brain scans, we can predict or explain certain behaviors. Some researchers say they can tell by an fMRI if that brain is lying, excited, afraid, bored, or brain-dead and put a general address on some major mental functions.

But it's not so simple to knock down and tie up brain function to one spot. Some call this an updated and computerized phrenology: phrenology with a computer and some really good pictures.

What these images actually show about your thoughts and feelings, say critics, is often overstated. For one thing, we don't really know what you are exactly thinking, feeling, or responding to when a certain part of your brain shows activity. Sure, we know what you *say* is going on in there, and some brain sections such as the amygdala are so specific we can guess that whatever excites it is some strong emotion quite probably related to fear. Or not. And that's only one problem.

The problems are not only with the lack of information about what these images really mean but also with how the data for brain scans are analyzed. In a paper originally titled "Voodoo Correlations in Social Neuroscience" (and changed on publication to "Puzzlingly High Correlations in fMRI Studies of Emotion, Personality, and Social Cognition"), Edward Vul and associates made some pointed criticisms of the way most fMRI research analyzes study results and reaches conclusions, especially about personality and behavior. They concluded that "a disturbingly large, and quite prominent, segment of fMRI research on emotion, personality, and social cognition is using seriously defective research methods and producing a profusion of numbers that should not be believed."

The Five Flaws of Brain Scans

Michael Shermer, the publisher of *Skeptic Magazine* (www.skeptic.com), agrees. Writing in *Scientific American Mind* about brain scans and emotion, he summarizes what an fMRI really can show, what it can't, and why it's a wonderful tool that can be used to reach some dubious conclusions.

Flaw #1: Studies Are Skewed by Selection and Environment
There's no doubt that fMRI studies are afflicted with a selection bias: the subject sample can't be completely random, because many people simply can't stand to be in the coffin-like confines long enough to have a brain scanned. Some 20 percent of experiment volunteers back out. In fact, Shermer volunteered to try it and says he developed claustrophobia and had to bail out of the experiment before it even started. So studies can't be said to fairly represent a randomized sample of brains.

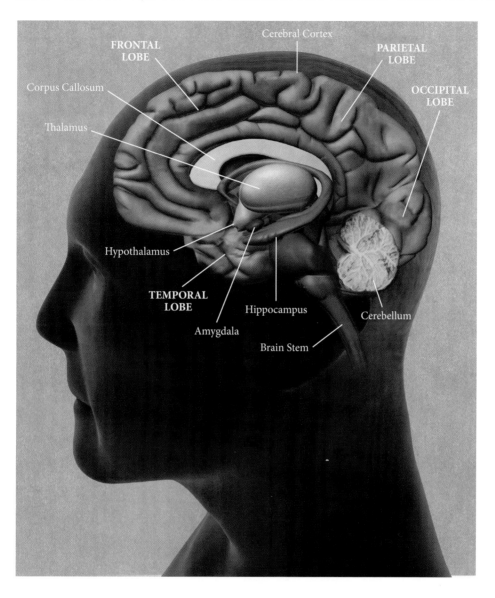

Some of Your Brain's Most Important Parts

Neuron

Axons

Neurotransmitter
Vesicles

Neurotransmitter
Molecules

Synapse

Receptors

Dendrites

Neurons: Your Brain Cells at Work

The axons are the long arms of neurons that send signals out; each neuron has one. Dendrites are the shorter, branched receivers; each neuron has many. Electrical signals and chemical messengers (neurotransmitters) leap the tiny gap (synapse) between neurons.

How the Brain Makes New Neurons

New cells in the brain are made from neural stem cells that divide periodically in two main areas: the ventricles (purple, inset), which contain cerebrospinal fluid to nourish the central nervous system, and the hippocampus (light blue, inset), crucial for learning and memory. The neural stem cells proliferate (cell pathways below) and give rise to other neural stem cells and to neural precursors that can grow up to be either neurons or glial cells. But these newborn neural stem cells need to move (red arrows, inset) away from their parents before they can differentiate. Only 50 percent, on average, survive; the others perish. In an adult brain, newborn neurons have been found in the hippocampus and the olfactory bulbs, which process smell. Researchers hope to be able to induce an adult brain to repair itself by coaxing neural stem cells or neural precursors to divide and develop when and where they are needed.

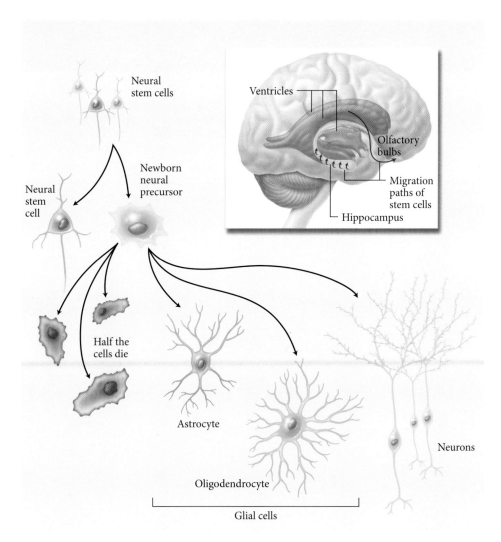

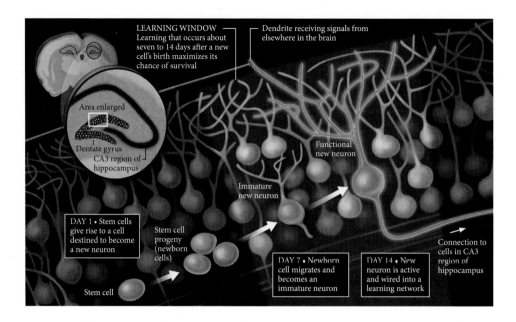

How Learning Helps Save New Neurons

During their first weeks of life, newborn brain cells in the hippocampus migrate from the edge of the dentate gyrus (where they are born) into a deeper area, where they mature and become wired into a network of neurons. Research shows that learning when the cells are about one to two weeks old enhances their survival. If there is no learning activity, most new hippocampus neurons die.

Epigenetics: Volume Control for Your Genes

The DNA sequence is not the only code stored in your chromosomes. Epigenetic information of several kinds can act like volume knobs to amplify or mute the effect of genes, or gene expression. This is encoded as chemical attachments to the DNA (or to the histone proteins that control its shape within the chromosomes). Your epigenome can be affected by your environment, your actions, and even your thoughts and feelings.

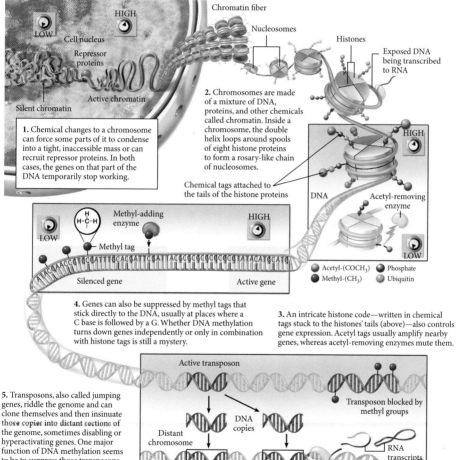

1. Chemical changes to a chromosome can force some parts of it to condense into a tight, inaccessible mass or can recruit repressor proteins. In both cases, the genes on that part of the DNA temporarily stop working.

2. Chromosomes are made of a mixture of DNA, proteins, and other chemicals called chromatin. Inside a chromosome, the double helix loops around spools of eight histone proteins to form a rosary-like chain of nucleosomes.

3. An intricate histone code—written in chemical tags stuck to the histones' tails (above)—also controls gene expression. Acetyl tags usually amplify nearby genes, whereas acetyl-removing enzymes mute them.

4. Genes can also be suppressed by methyl tags that stick directly to the DNA, usually at places where a C base is followed by a G. Whether DNA methylation turns down genes independently or only in combination with histone tags is still a mystery.

5. Transposons, also called jumping genes, riddle the genome and can clone themselves and then insinuate those copies into distant sections of the genome, sometimes disabling or hyperactivating genes. One major function of DNA methylation seems to be to suppress those transposons, which make up almost half the human genome.

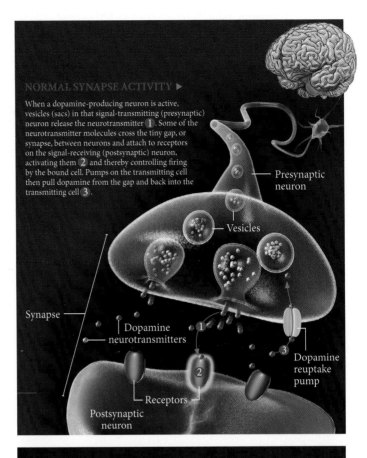

When a dopamine-producing neuron is active, vesicles (sacs) in that signal-transmitting (presynaptic) neuron release the neurotransmitter ①. Some of the neurotransmitter molecules cross the tiny gap, or synapse, between neurons and attach to receptors on the signal-receiving (postsynaptic) neuron, activating them ② and thereby controlling firing by the bound cell. Pumps on the transmitting cell then pull dopamine from the gap and back into the transmitting cell ③.

Presynaptic neuron

Vesicles

Synapse

Dopamine neurotransmitters

Dopamine reuptake pump

Receptors

Postsynaptic neuron

▼ DRUG-ENHANCED SYNAPSE ACTIVITY

Drugs such as methylphenidate (Ritalin and Concerta, for example) block the reuptake of dopamine. More dopamine is available to attach to a postsynaptic neuron, which amplifies the strength of the signal transmitted from the presynaptic neuron.

Adderall and other amphetamines enter the presynaptic neuron through the pumping mechanism and cause dopamine to be displaced into the synaptic gap, increasing the amount of neurotransmitter available to act on the postsynaptic cell.

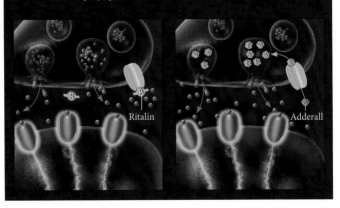

Ritalin

Adderall

How Brain Enhancers Work (left)

Some purported enhancers, such as the drugs methylphenidate and amphetamines, alter the activity of the neurotransmitter dopamine in the synapses, the junction between neurons. Enhanced dopamine signaling may improve learning by focusing attention and interest on a task.

The Memory Code: A Seat of Memory

A region of the hippocampus called CA1 (shown here in the human brain) is important to forming memories of events and places. To gain insight into the process, researchers developed a way to record the activity of more than two hundred individual neurons simultaneously in the CA1 region in the brains of mice.

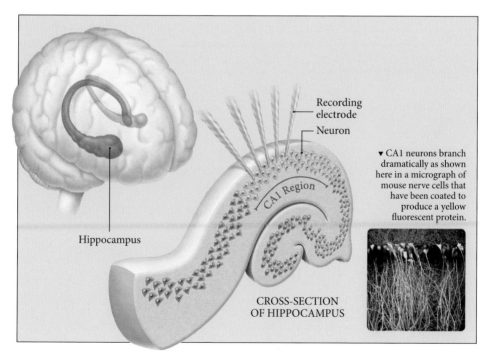

Recording electrode

Neuron

CA1 Region

▼ CA1 neurons branch dramatically as shown here in a micrograph of mouse nerve cells that have been coated to produce a yellow fluorescent protein.

Hippocampus

CROSS-SECTION OF HIPPOCAMPUS

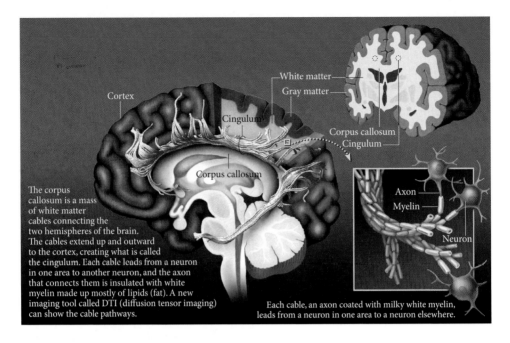

Cortex

Cingulum

Corpus callosum

White matter
Gray matter

Corpus callosum
Cingulum

Axon
Myelin

Neuron

The corpus callosum is a mass of white matter cables connecting the two hemispheres of the brain. The cables extend up and outward to the cortex, creating what is called the cingulum. Each cable leads from a neuron in one area to another neuron, and the axon that connects them is insulated with white myelin made up mostly of lipids (fat). A new imaging tool called DTI (diffusion tensor imaging) can show the cable pathways.

Each cable, an axon coated with milky white myelin, leads from a neuron in one area to a neuron elsewhere.

What Is White Matter?

White matter fills nearly half the human brain with millions of cables (white) that connect brain cells (gray) in differing parts of the brain, rather like trunk lines connecting telephones across a country.

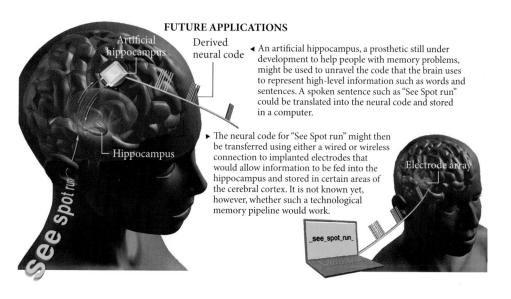

FUTURE APPLICATIONS

◄ An artificial hippocampus, a prosthetic still under development to help people with memory problems, might be used to unravel the code that the brain uses to represent high-level information such as words and sentences. A spoken sentence such as "See Spot run" could be translated into the neural code and stored in a computer.

► The neural code for "See Spot run" might then be transferred using either a wired or wireless connection to implanted electrodes that would allow information to be fed into the hippocampus and stored in certain areas of the cerebral cortex. It is not known yet, however, whether such a technological memory pipeline would work.

An Artificial Hippocampus

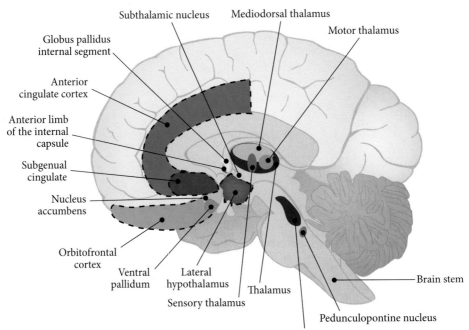

Subthalamic nucleus   Mediodorsal thalamus

Globus pallidus
internal segment

Motor thalamus

Anterior
cingulate cortex

Anterior limb
of the internal
capsule

Subgenual
cingulate

Nucleus
accumbens

Orbitofrontal
cortex

Ventral   Lateral
pallidum   hypothalamus   Thalamus

Sensory thalamus

Brain stem

Pedunculopontine nucleus

Periventricular gray/periaqueductal gray

NOTE: Dashed regions are on the
midline; others are at different depths.

DISORDER	ESTABLISHED SITES	PROMISING SITES	POTENTIAL SITES
Parkinson's disease	Motor thalamus, globus pallidus internal segment, subthalamic nucleus, pedunculopontine nucleus		
Dystonia	Globus pallidus internal segment		
Essential tremor	Motor thalamus		
Depression		Subgenual cingulate, nucleus accumbens	Orbitofrontal cortex, anterior cingulate cortex, ventral pallidum, mediodorsal thalamus
Pain	Periventricular gray/peraqueductal gray, sensory thalamus		Orbitofrontal cortex, anterior cingulate cortex
Obsessive-compulsive disorder	Anterior limb of the internal capsule		
Cluster headache	Lateral hypothalamus		
Minimally conscious			Thalamus

Sparking Recovery with Brain Pacemakers (left)

The first puzzle for neurosurgeons attempting to treat patients with deep-brain stimulation is figuring out where in the brain to place the electrode. Much of this work is done through animal experimentation. Noninvasive brain scans of people with various disorders also offer clues to which brain areas are involved in controlling the problematic behaviors and sensations.

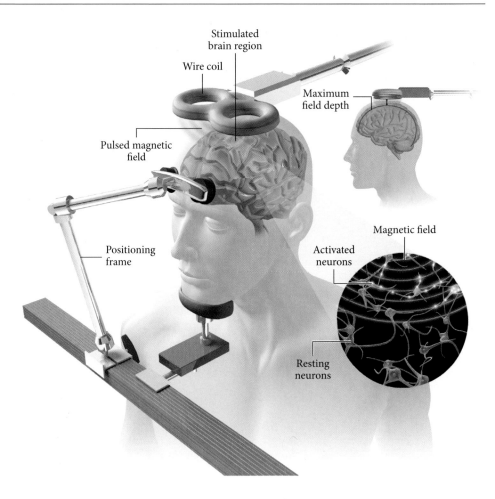

Targeted Magnetic Brain Stimulation

Transcranial magnetic stimulation (TMS) is effective for treating some depression. A coil near the subject's scalp sends a powerful and rapidly changing magnetic field safely and painlessly through skin and bone. Each brief pulse, lasting only microseconds, contains little energy, but the precisely located field induces electric current in nearby neurons, thus activating targeted regions of the brain (bottom right). Because the strength of the magnetic field falls off rapidly with distance, it can penetrate only a few centimeters to the outer cortex of the brain (top right). A principal benefit of TMS is that it requires no direct electrical connection to the body (as is required for electroconvulsive therapy), is painless, and has few side effects.

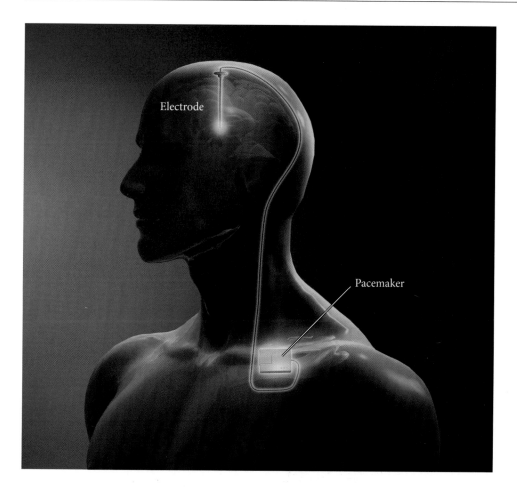

Electrode

Pacemaker

The Future of Optogenetic Brain Stimulation

The emerging field of optogenetics, which combines genetic engineering with light, might eventually replace electrode-based deep-brain stimulation (DBS) as a way of treating Parkinson's disease, among other disorders. In optogenetics, proteins delivered to problem areas would be stimulated by light to become active and change neuron activity. DBS stimulates parts of the brain that control movement with a "pacemaker" and an embedded electrode, which looks much like this illustration, to block nerve signals causing tremors and other symptoms of Parkinson's disease. Optogenetic stimulation can potentially target problem cells much more precisely than the electrodes used in DBS. But to get the right cells to make the light-sensitive protein, optogenetic treatment would require that patients undergo gene therapy, which is currently banned because of safety concerns.

An Artificial Retina

Dozens of people with damaged photoreceptor cells are being fitted with a device that consists of a small camera on eyeglasses, a belt-worn videoprocessor, and an array of electrodes implanted on the retina. Images are converted into patterns of light and dark and transmitted to the electrodes, which send signals through the optic nerve to the brain to form an image of light and dark patches and give useful sight.

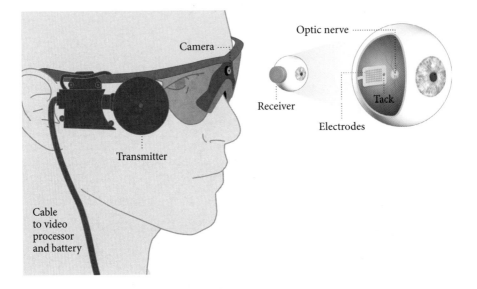

Spinal Cord Responsibilities (right)

Mending the spinal cord is a major research goal. More than 200,000 Americans have spinal cord damage, a number that, ironically, has grown because of improved acute care in the hours immediately following injury. Scientists are reluctant to raise false hopes, but research is ongoing. It is known that some severed spinal cord nerve cells do begin to extend new fingers, and bionic implants and brain stimulation may also help restore some functions.

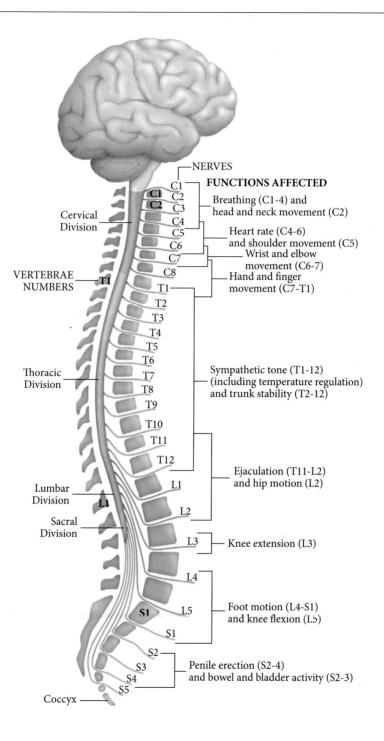

NERVES

FUNCTIONS AFFECTED

C1
C2
C3
C4
C5
C6
C7
C8

Breathing (C1-4) and
head and neck movement (C2)

Heart rate (C4-6)
and shoulder movement (C5)

Wrist and elbow
movement (C6-7)

Hand and finger
movement (C7-T1)

Cervical
Division

C1
C2

VERTEBRAE
NUMBERS

T1

T1
T2
T3
T4
T5
T6
T7
T8
T9
T10
T11
T12

Thoracic
Division

Sympathetic tone (T1-12)
(including temperature regulation)
and trunk stability (T2-12)

Ejaculation (T11-L2)
and hip motion (L2)

Lumbar
Division

L1

L1
L2
L3

Knee extension (L3)

Sacral
Division

L4
L5

Foot motion (L4-S1)
and knee flexion (L5)

S1

S1
S2
S3
S4
S5

Penile erection (S2-4)
and bowel and bladder activity (S2-3)

Coccyx

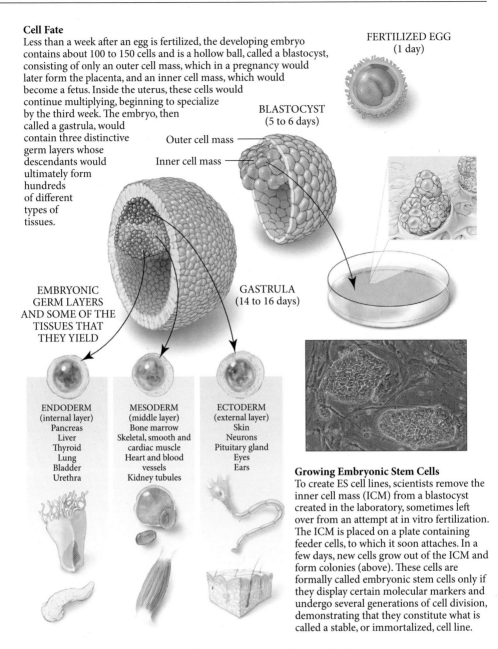

Cell Fate

Less than a week after an egg is fertilized, the developing embryo contains about 100 to 150 cells and is a hollow ball, called a blastocyst, consisting of only an outer cell mass, which in a pregnancy would later form the placenta, and an inner cell mass, which would become a fetus. Inside the uterus, these cells would continue multiplying, beginning to specialize by the third week. The embryo, then called a gastrula, would contain three distinctive germ layers whose descendants would ultimately form hundreds of different types of tissues.

FERTILIZED EGG
(1 day)

BLASTOCYST
(5 to 6 days)

Outer cell mass

Inner cell mass

EMBRYONIC
GERM LAYERS
AND SOME OF THE
TISSUES THAT
THEY YIELD

GASTRULA
(14 to 16 days)

ENDODERM
(internal layer)
Pancreas
Liver
Thyroid
Lung
Bladder
Urethra

MESODERM
(middle layer)
Bone marrow
Skeletal, smooth and
cardiac muscle
Heart and blood
vessels
Kidney tubules

ECTODERM
(external layer)
Skin
Neurons
Pituitary gland
Eyes
Ears

Growing Embryonic Stem Cells

To create ES cell lines, scientists remove the inner cell mass (ICM) from a blastocyst created in the laboratory, sometimes left over from an attempt at in vitro fertilization. The ICM is placed on a plate containing feeder cells, to which it soon attaches. In a few days, new cells grow out of the ICM and form colonies (above). These cells are formally called embryonic stem cells only if they display certain molecular markers and undergo several generations of cell division, demonstrating that they constitute what is called a stable, or immortalized, cell line.

The Origins and Fates of Embryonic Stem Cells

Embryonic stem (ES) cells are a controversial but proven source of valuable stem cells. They are derived from the part of a very-early-stage embryo that would eventually develop into an entire body. Because ES cells originate in this primordial stage, they retain the "pluripotent" ability to form any cell type in the body.

And when you read popular accounts of subjects who had their brains scanned while they were shopping, for example, realize that they were not walking around a Wal-Mart with head gear on. Far from it: they were jammed into a narrow tube with head locked firmly in place and subjected to loud rhythmic banging while they watched images, made choices, or experienced emotions. (One can only imagine the logistics of sexual activity studied under these conditions. On second thought, let's not.)

Flaw #2: Scans Don't Measure Direct Brain Activity

Popular accounts of fMRI research frequently describe how specific parts of the brain "light up" when the person is thinking about money or sex or God or what to buy from the Shopping Network. Indeed, Shermer notes, *Scientific American* authors have been guilty of repeating this oversimplification.

But an fMRI is not a direct image of your brain showing mental activity. It's an image created through indirectly measuring the flow of oxygenated blood and then correlating that information to something you are doing or thinking at the time, and the blood flow response takes time. So it's a stretch to say there is cause and effect and to relate this blood surge to a specific activity.

Flaw #3: The Pretty Colors Are Fake

Nothing sells a brain study like an image splotched with sharply defined and brightly colored brain regions. This is highly misleading, Shermer writes, because it suggests well-defined processing areas in the brain, when in fact the neural activity may be distributed in more of a loosely defined network.

Scientists agree as a basic principle that changes in blood flow and oxygenation levels in particular areas of the brain signal greater neural activity. But the coloring is artificial, and the process of coloring the regions is even more misleading, because differences in activity levels are tiny. The choice of what to emphasize may also be misleading. Shermer quotes one researcher in referring to the cingulate nucleus, an area dealing with conflict: "You can get it to respond by showing subjects a picture of, say, Hillary Clinton. But the cingulate nucleus does fifty-seven other things as well."

Finally, scientists know that most brain activity is not stimulus driven; it is spontaneous. We don't know why there is so much activity and what it is doing. In other words, many areas of the brain are continually active during different processing tasks, and separating them out properly is a challenge that requires careful experimental design.

Flaw #4: That's Not One Brain: That's a Statistic

The next time you see one of those colorful brain scans with an arrow pointing to some spot that says, "This is your brain on X," know that the image usually does not represent any one person's brain. It's a statistical computation of all of the brains scanned in that study, rendered with artificial colors to highlight the places where there is a consistent response to a given task or experimental condition.

Remember how the scanner snaps pictures of rapid-fire brain activity every two seconds, resulting in hundreds to thousands of images per scanning period? Researchers adjust data, make corrections for head motion and for small differences in the different brains, and convert it into an image.

The scientists line up all the individual images with one another and then combine the data and take averages for the subjects in the experiment. They employ additional statistical software to convert raw data into images, as well as to correct for other possible intervening variables, such as cognitive tasks that produce neural activity changes in the brain faster than the blood flow changes that are actually being measured by the MRI.

Flaw #5: There Are Many Reasons That Area Activates

Interpreting brain scan activity is as much an art as a science at this point, says Shermer. It's tempting to look at one of those spots and say, "This is where X happens in your brain," when in fact that area could be lighting up when involved in all sorts of tasks.

For example, your right prefrontal cortex lights up when you do almost any difficult task. So when you are engaged in thinking about

DO YOU SEE WHAT I SEE?

Scientists say they have figured out a way to know what you are looking at—sort of. Researchers at the University of California, Berkeley, have developed a method to decode the patterns in visual areas of the brain to figure out what someone has seen. Using fMRI to record activity in the visual cortices of volunteers while they looked at a series of images, the researchers inferred what image that person was looking at by monitoring activity in different sections of the brain and then deciphering what information would most likely be found in the corresponding part of the visual field. The method, however, is limited to information that can be clearly represented mathematically, such as pictures, sounds, and movements. Their work showed up in a *Scientific American* article (Swaminathan, 2008).

something specific, there is a network of several different areas involved in communicating with one another, and the prefrontal cortex may be involved. It also becomes active when engaged in one particular task. Teasing these differences apart requires making relative comparisons across a spectrum of tasks.

Certain experiments work especially well with fMRI because decisions provide contrasts between tasks, giving the neuroscientist something to compare. But many activities don't. The amygdala, an area typically associated with processing the fear response, is also activated by arousal and positive emotions. So that doesn't mean that every time your amygdala lights up, you are experiencing fear. Every brain area lights up under lots of different states. We just don't have the data to tell us how selectively active an area is.

What's Next? And What About My Brain?

MRI technology has had such a tremendous impact that it's hard to believe it is still very new: the first MRI performed on a human was in 1974, and fMRI technology is less than twenty years old.

VIRTUALLY THERE: INSIDE YOUR BODY
AND BRAIN IN 3-D VIDEO

A new imaging technology could give doctors unprecedented noninvasive access to the interior of the body and help them plan safer, more effective treatments and surgeries.

The technology combines data from CT, MRI, and PET scans and channels the information into a single computer to generate detailed images of the inside of a brain and body and project a three-dimensional hologram onto a screen. Using special 3-D glasses and a video game controller, doctors can then travel virtually under the skin, past bones, and through the arteries and blood vessels, maneuvering around organs in all directions.

They can see anatomical obstacles that could cause problems in surgery and even simulate surgery to practice a technique or to see how removing parts of an organ might affect the patient. This technology can make radiation therapy more precise, and in the near future, surgeons will be able to take the technology into the operating room and go directly to the area they mapped out the day before and perform the surgery with great precision.

"This will take surgical planning to a whole new level," says E. Brian Butler, chairman of radiation oncology at Methodist Hospital in Houston and creator of the technology. Butler calls the new technique "Plato's cave," in a nod to Plato's "Allegory of the Cave." In this story, prisoners in a cave saw shadows on the wall as reality. One day a prisoner escaped and actually saw the outside world and an expanded reality. In much the same way, Butler said, his new visual approach to medicine opens up a whole new world for physicians and patients. It's also yet another example of cooperation among many sciences: it weds computer science and engineering to biology and anatomy, a partnership becoming increasingly common in advancing medicine and medical research.

The technology is improving at a phenomenal rate. Very small MRIs are under development. Scanners that can be placed on a limb are in use now, and researchers are looking at ways to use MRIs to predict strokes or to see them in the earliest stages. Such images could also tell us when a brain needs a boost for improved functioning and where to deliver it in terms of an electrical stimulation, site-specific drugs, or other means.

Different technology is being studied to develop ever smaller MRI-type imagers: handheld machines to read brains at accident scenes (and at security checkpoints) might be next.

Suddenly, the medical gadgets that Dr. Leonard "Bones" McKoy used in the original *Star Trek* TV series in the 1960s don't seem so far-fetched. In the series, set in the future years of the 2260s, McKoy had a psychotricorder to scan and record past memories; a neural neutralizer to remove thoughts related to criminal acts; a K-3 indicator to measure the level of pain as indicated through neural activity; and a brain-circuitry pattern, a diagnostic tool to map the unique neural activity of an individual for identification. Some of these will no doubt be reality in a lot fewer than two hundred years.

Other methods may offer a view of your inner brain. We already have pill-size cameras that are swallowed and then broadcast images of the territory as they travel through the digestive system. It's a matter of scale and technology to create similar tools for the brain, some say.

As for uses of this technology in the very near future, there's little doubt that brain scans will find their way into everything from the classroom to the courtroom, and possibly the bedroom, say legal experts.

Some potential uses are bound to create interesting new lawsuits and legislation. The brains of our children from toddlers to college students could be imaged to select the best educational methods or tools for them or their potential for some careers over others. Or they could be used in questionable ways to see if in fact they are college material at all or acceptable material for certain insurance policies—or perhaps better suited for prison (see "Neuroethics," p. 129).

Agents of commerce and politics might want access to brain scanning to see what people select in political candidates (liberal or conservative?) and sodas (Coke or Pepsi?). Insurers, employers, security firms, divorce lawyers, and perhaps dating services could want to use this so-called mind-reading technology to determine truthfulness, suitability for the task at hand, and even adherence to the American Way: Big Brother is very very interested. The military and intelligence communities have a big stake in being able to know what you are thinking, and the U.S. Defense Advanced Research Projects Agency has budgeted millions to study and design related technology, including technology to enable soldiers on the battlefield to communicate using computer-mediated telepathy. The aim is to analyze neural signals that exist in the brain before words are spoken and transmit— or intercept—them.

But the primary uses of these magical machines will still be diagnosis and treatment. They are and will continue to be invaluable tools for helping to repair your brain and keep it healthy.

CHAPTER SIX

Rewiring the Brain Electric

IN BRIEF

We've known electricity can change our brains since at least A.D. 43, when a court physician to the Roman Emperor Claudius reported soothing headaches with the touch of the electrically charged torpedo fish. Over the centuries since, scientists have confirmed that the brain is indeed an electrical organ, and that one way neurons communicate with one another is through electrical impulses. But until now, only science fiction has imagined how and to what extent that knowledge, coupled with technology, could radically change treatments for some dreaded neurological conditions.

𝕿𝖍𝖊𝖓: The brain uses electricity and can be changed by electrical current, usually by interrupting memory and thought with electroshock therapy applied to the entire brain.

ᴎᴏᴡ: Targeted techniques for delivering mild electrical and magnetic charges painlessly to (and into) specific parts of the brain are effective treatments for movement disorders and depression, and are being hotly pursued as therapies for other brain-based ills.

Tomorrow: It seems that virtually anything wrong with your brain might be fixed with a jolt of electricity—or a zap to the right spot might jump-start creativity, provoke brain cell production, and repair stroke damage.

The Electrical Revolution: A History of Hot-Wiring Your Head

It's been a long, controversial, and somewhat messy journey from those first glimmerings about the brain electric to today's successful brain stimulation treatments.

Scientists of yore were fascinated by electricity, and for hundreds of years, they have been applying electrical charges to the brain to treat (or make a stab at treating) various ills. Some discoveries have been eagerly embraced. For nearly a century, we've able to detect brain impulses without cutting into the skull by using electroencephalography (EEGs) to measure electrical activity along the scalp to record brain action. It's still a diagnostic tool for epilepsy.

But messing with the mind electric has been off-putting, especially in the past century when Swiss physiologist Walter Rudolf Hess showed he could prompt behaviors such as rage, hunger, and sleepiness in cats by electrically stimulating parts of their brains with wires. Then electroshock appeared around the 1930s and became a popular, though controversial, treatment from 1949 on through the 1950s for just about any kind of mental disturbance.

ELECTROSHOCK'S SHOCKING HISTORY

Electroshock (also called electroconvulsive shock therapy, for disturbing reasons) triggers brief seizures from an external electrical charge that interrupt the brain's conversations with itself. It causes changes in brain chemistry that ease symptoms of schizophrenia, deep depression, and other mental illnesses. It is still considered an effective and appropriate treatment for severe depression and bipolar disorders that don't respond to other means. Novelist, screenwriter, and actor Carrie Fisher, for example, is one of many who say they have found it of tremendous benefit. Nevertheless, it's considered a crude instrument compared to the more precise effects from newer techniques.

Electroshock therapy of the past was controversial because of the brutality of some of the treatments, which used high charges resulting in permanent memory loss and sometimes death, and because of public perceptions of it as an extreme and cruel treatment. In some popular books and films, it appears as a punitive treatment for uncooperative mental patients, as in *One Flew over the Cuckoo's Nest*. It was linked in the minds of many with lobotomy, in which the frontal lobes are surgically destroyed—another popular and drastic treatment for the mentally ill that, incidentally, won a Nobel Prize in 1949.

Yet it remains for some people the only hope of relieving devastating depression or severe mental illnesses and is used in controlled treatments.

Neurosurgical pioneers began refining electrical stimulation in the 1950s, targeting mild electricity to the brains of people suffering from chronic pain, depression, and movement disorders. But the technology wasn't up to it. Batteries available then were much too large to be implanted, the devices were awkward, and the relief was sporadic.

In the 1970s, there was more controversy after neuroscientist José Delgados implanted radio-equipped electrodes into animals (and some humans) and showed he could control their actions with the push of a button. He proved his technique with a spectacular experiment in which he stopped a charging bull by flicking a handheld switch that send a jolt of electricity into an electrode in the bull's brain.

The implications of mind control were ominous to many, fueled even more by some scandalous experiments in which researchers tried to change a homosexual's sexual orientation with brain electrodes and by a proposal by some scientists to use brain stimulation or psychosurgery on blacks who were rioting in inner cities.

Coupled with the bad feelings about electroshock and lobotomy, messing with the mind surgically and electrically fell out of favor. By the 1980s brain-stimulation studies bogged down in ethical controversies and funding issues, and many researchers drifted to psychopharmacology, which seemed then to be a much safer, more effective way to treat brain disorders than brain stimulation or surgery.

The Current Brain Research: Magnets to Implants

Brain stimulation got hot again recently amid the growing recognition of the limits and perils of drugs for treating many brain ailments. Implant research was boosted by the tremendous advances in computers, electrodes, microelectronics, and brain-scanning technologies and by miniaturization of these and of batteries.

Research on humans today is tightly controlled, unlike the wild frontier experiments of the past, and researchers have come up with several ways to use electricity painlessly and effectively to change the brain.

Today the more advanced technology of electrifying the brain is accepted treatment for movement-related nerve disorders, and researchers are finding it can do much more. Deep brain stimulation (DBS) has shown tantalizing promise for a host of psychiatric disorders, including severe cases of depression, chronic pain, obsessive-compulsive disorder, attention deficit hyperactivity disorder, vision problems, and Tourette's syndrome, and it has been attempted as a cure for anorexia and obesity—just about anything that involves the brain.

Consider the brain pacemaker. Documented in action in a brief video, it's reality TV as riveting as anything you'll ever see. A man with Parkinson's disease in his mid-fifties, affable and articulate, faces the camera and talks a bit about a medical procedure he's had. He holds in his hand what looks like a remote control.

"I'll turn myself off now," he says mildly. The man presses a button on the control, a beep sounds, and his right arm starts to shake, then to flap violently. It's as if a biological hurricane has engulfed him. With effort, the man grasps the malfunctioning right arm with his left hand and slowly, firmly, subdues the commotion, as if he were calming a child in the throes of a temper tantrum. He's breathing hard, and it's clear he can't keep it up much longer. With an almost desperate gesture, he reaches out for the controller and manages to press the button again. There's a soft beep, and suddenly it's over. He's fine.

The man in the video is one of tens of thousands of patients who are benefiting from implanted electrodes and DBS. He's a patient of neuroscientists Morton L. Kringelbach and Tipu Z. Aziz, who hold appointments at the University of Oxford and other research centers, and who wrote the previous pacemaker description. They are pioneers in the startling world of brain pacemakers.

As recently as 1972, such "cures" were the stuff of science fiction—specifically *The Terminal Man*, a film in which surgeons implant electrodes in the brain of a man with epilepsy and connect them to a miniature computer in his chest to control the seizures. Back then, we didn't have the knowledge of brain anatomy or the miniaturized technology to make such a treatment work dependably.

The Terminal Man

Based on a 1972 novel by Michael Crichton, the 1974 film features a genius computer programmer who has epileptic seizures in which he blacks out, commits violent crimes, and comes to with no knowledge of his acts. Surgeons implant electrodes in his brain and connect them to a miniature computer in his chest to control the seizures. But the patient has an irrational phobia about computers overtaking the world, the violence escalates, and he kills and is finally killed. In the more complex book plot, one of the implanted electrodes provokes sexual pleasure along with seizures, which leads the patient to initiate more seizures. Crichton, a Harvard-trained doctor, studied with one of the first (and controversial) brain implant researchers before he wrote this book.

There's promise of even more tomorrow. The wiring of the brain is such that scientists think an electrical jolt in just the right spot might stimulate the growth of new neurons, spark lost memories, or reverse Alzheimer's disease. Hypothetically it seems there is little that goes wrong with the brain that could not benefit from some electrical intervention.

Most of these treatments are still experimental, however, and many, such as rewiring a brain stricken by stroke or dementia, are still the stuff of science fiction. But thousands of people have had electrical brain therapy of some sort or are walking around with electrodes in their heads that help them function.

More than forty thousand people worldwide have electrodes installed deep in the brain to quell epilepsy, Parkinson's disease, and other movement-related disorders. Connected to a pacemaker-like implanted battery, they can flip a switch to stop tremors and convulsions. Thousands more, who were wheelchair bound because of a disabling movement disorder called dystonia, have been able to walk and lead nearly normal lives.

More than seven hundred people have had electrical brain stimulation for otherwise treatment-resistant pain, and a small number of people getting experimental DBS have found immediate relief for severe depression, phantom limb pain, cluster headaches, obsessive-compulsive disorder, Tourette's syndrome, and just about any other kind of brain-centered dysfunction.

The market for these brain treatments is enormous and growing. More than 10 million Americans struggle with major depression, and more than 3 million have spinal cord injuries, have amyotrophic lateral sclerosis and stroke, or are legally blind. Some 5.3 million suffer from memory loss connected with Alzheimer's disease, a number that's expected to rise to 100 million worldwide by midcentury, especially in an aging population. Wounded warriors are returning from battle with severe depression, brain damage, paralysis, and lost limbs.

Transcranial magnetic stimulation (TMS) is FDA approved for depression, and has the advantage of being noninvasive. (It's also been

TODAY'S TREATMENTS FOR CHARGING YOUR BRAIN

In the future, electrical treatments might stimulate neuron growth (to help with memory or repair damage), creativity (by stimulating more activity in the right hemisphere), or wakefulness and focus.

Today's electrical therapies include these:

- *Transcranial magnetic stimulation (TMS).* A magnetic field focused from outside the skull influences electrical signals in specific parts of the brain. It's painless, approved by the FDA for treating depression, and may quiet epileptic convulsions and Parkinson's disease tremors.
- *Electroshock therapy (EST).* It got a bad reputation from some brutal and inappropriate applications in the past, but is still used today in a controlled form for severe depression (see "Electroshock's Shocking History," p. 89).
- *Deep brain stimulation (DBS).* Extremely thin electrodes (wires) implanted in specific parts of the brain use electricity to stimulate brain activity or interrupt it. They may be connected to a computer or a pacemaker-like battery and have a switch to turn the power off or on.
- *Radio-controlled or amplified electrodes.* Sometimes erroneously called "brain chips," these are connected to and communicate with a computer to translate thoughts into action (see "Your Bionic Brain," p. 101).
- *Functional electrical stimulation (FES).* This gives light electrical shocks to paralyzed muscles to make them move, thus sending messages to the brain to help it rewire itself and relearn how to move the affected muscles.

know to trigger savant-like mathematical abilities or deep religious experience in ordinary people.) However, the effects are not always permanent.

Another noninvasive treatment showing promise for helping stroke patients regain activity in areas of their damaged brains even three years after a stroke—a period in which no improvement has been expected—is dual-hemisphere transcranial direct current stimulation (tDCS). This technique uses electrical stimulation to modulate brain activity at the same time the limb affected by the stroke is getting occupational therapy. After only five treatment sessions, researchers saw significant improvement in motor function. Functional magnetic resonance imaging also showed increased brain activity in brain areas that control limb movement on the affected side.

But the most sizzling new therapy is deep brain stimulation. Over the past decade, it's been recognized as an astoundingly effective treatment to quell Parkinson's disease and other movement-related disorders. The treatment, essentially a pacemaker for the brain, consists of a deceptively simple two-part device. A surgeon threads one or two thin wires into carefully selected locations deep within the brain and connects them to a small battery inserted just underneath the skin near the collarbone. Pulses of electricity travel from the battery to electrodes at the tip of each wire to interrupt, amplify, or correct dysfunctional electrical activity that's causing medical problems. Doctors can tailor the speed, strength, and length of the pulses to get the desired result.

Since the 1990s, tens of thousands have benefited: the average long-term success rate is 60 to 70 percent, and when doctors are skilled in patient selection, the success rate approaches 100 percent. Thanks to research and technology that makes batteries as small as the ones in cell phones, more than 250 hospitals in the United States alone perform DBS for movement disorders.

The new technology gives DBS huge advantages over most other kinds of neurosurgery: it doesn't change the physical structure of the brain, and it's reversible. If the electrodes malfunction or simply don't work, they can be turned off or removed. Because the brain surface has no feeling, patients are awake and aware during the surgery and can respond to surgeons to help prevent damage to important brain functions.

Recently electrodes have become safer, the batteries smaller and longer lasting, and advances in brain-imaging techniques such as magnetic resonance imaging have made it possible to place electrodes with greater precision.

The effects are instantaneous. They usually appear while the patient is still on the operating table. And taming movement disorders is just the beginning.

Discovering Depression's Sweet Spot

A few years ago, neuroscientist Helen Mayberg stunned the neurological community by reversing severe depression with DBS to a specific spot in the brain.

Mayberg, then at Johns Hopkins University, and Wayne C. Drevets, then at Washington University Medical School, had already independently discovered a depression-related place in the brain: Brodmann area 25, in the cerebral cortex. She and colleagues at the University of Toronto then cured eight of twelve spectacularly depressed people—people whose crippling depression had defied years of treatment with drugs, talk therapy, and even electroshock therapy. The cure was against all odds, and they did it with implants and stimulation to Brodmann area 25, which appears to connect several brain regions involved in mood, thought, and emotion and is hyperactive in depressed patients.

Suddenly the DBS stampede was on. Now it's being studied as a treatment for everything neuro, especially mental illness. And with some reason.

But Mayberg is more cautious. Scientists still don't know why calming area 25 has such an effect, she says, and many factors are involved in mental illness, from neurochemistry to genetics to environment. Moreover, a complex network links thought and mood, including the cortex and the limbic regions where the fear-inducing amygdala lives. Using DTI technology, she and others are also finding that the tracts connected to depression vary among individuals.

So before we get too excited about DBS for short-circuiting mental illness, there are formidable obstacles to overcome.

DBS is effective for disorders in which a precise brain area can be targeted, such as Parkinson's disease and epilepsy. But its uses for more complex mental illnesses are still experimental. The problem is that DBS is a relatively blunt tool: it's an on-off switch, either inhibiting or exciting a brain region (and, in turn, the other brain structures that region talks to). That's fine for Parkinson's disease, in which an overactive brain area may need quieting and in which the brain areas involved are distinct.

But there's no off-on area for most mental ailments. They are much more complex and individual. Not enough is known about the interaction of brain networks and biochemistry that contribute to mental illness. And because it involves precise and expensive brain surgery, it's unlikely brain implants will be used for any but the most severe cases, at least in the near future. So far, DBS has been applied to fewer than fifty depressed patients, and although it may become approved by the FDA for depression in the next few years, Mayberg doesn't think it will be a common treatment.

Could Implants Help Alzheimer's Patients?

There's been some optimism about brain implants for Alzheimer's disease. But in this disease, neurons die, stop functioning, or lose their connections to one another and can no longer store memories. It is unlikely that DBS could repair such intricate connections, but brain chips of the future might (see "Your Bionic Brain," p. 101).

It's not an easy surgery, it's not a cure, and the procedure has risks. It's an exact and delicate surgery, and the first puzzle for neurosurgeons is figuring out precisely where in the brain to place the electrode to affect only the neurons related to the condition being treated, without causing side effects by accidentally activating the wrong spot. DBS doesn't sharpen or revive mental functions or stop the disease from progressing; and it can affect adjacent parts of the brain, which can lead to deafness, speech disorders, and balance problems.

TURN IT UP, DEAR, AND TURN ME ON

In his 1973 film *Sleeper,* Woody Allen predicted that people of the future won't bother to get all sweaty and personal for sex: they'll just step into an Orgasmatron, where (presumably) a pleasure center in the brain will be stimulated by signals that zap just the right spot.

It's not so far-fetched. A pain control doctor has discovered how electrical current provokes orgasms and has trademarked the name Orgasmatron. The doctor, Stuart Meloy, a North Carolina physician who specializes in implanting spinal electrodes to alleviate pain, found by chance that a slightly off-kilter placement caused one woman to exclaim, "You're going to have to teach my husband to do that."

Meloy ran a small FDA-approved pilot trial and in 2006 reported that ten of eleven women who stopped having or never had had orgasms experienced sexual arousal with the temporary implant. Of that group, four were able to experience orgasm.

On his Web site, Meloy calls the use of spinal cord stimulation to treat orgasmic dysfunction *neurally augmented sexual function.* But so far there isn't a sex chip, and it may never become a practical means of adding the buzz back in anyone's love life. Still, it's nice to see someone working on a sex aid for women.

What's Next? And What About My Brain?

There's a tremendous future for manipulating the current in your head. There are obstacles, of course, but such rewiring holds promise for treating, and improving, your brain.

Here's the wish list from researchers looking at electrical brain stimulation:

- Find the neural networks contributing to serious mental illness and the right charge needed to ease symptoms without affecting the rest of the brain.

- Develop "smart" brain pacemakers that can sense an irregular neurological pattern and respond with the exact impulse needed to avert a problem or send an alarm.
- Help people with severe paralysis (or locked-in syndrome, in which the brain and mind remain clear while the body is paralyzed) to communicate or even move limbs by installing microprocessors directly in the brain to relay electrical impulses to nerves.
- Stimulate production of new brain cells in healthy or sick brains to boost brain activity and replace damaged or missing neurons.
- Stimulate creativity by equalizing the output of both brain hemispheres or by beefing up the right (so-called creative) hemisphere.

But despite the impressive recent advances, electrical brain stimulation still has a ways to go. First, we don't know enough yet about the brain's function, activity, and wiring, so scientists don't completely understand how it works. They do know that the pulses sent to the electrodes sometimes drive and sometimes inhibit the natural activity of neurons and that sometimes they hit the spot for an intended effect—and sometimes not.

Second, we need better technology. The tiny electrodes aren't tiny enough yet. The electrode used for Parkinson's disease is only about a millimeter and a half wide, but it straddles up to 1 million neurons packed tightly within the brain. It's tricky to banish the symptoms without injuring other neurons or damaging blood vessels: 1 to 3 percent of patients have bleeding that leads to a stroke.

Moreover, today's DBS devices are relatively crude and simplistic. The battery sends constant, unchanging pulses that the surgical team tailors to the precise strength, frequency, and duration that will best ease the patient's symptoms when installed. After that, the battery is set to run indefinitely and doesn't vary in signal strength or pattern.

In the future, a smart device could respond with the exact impulse and only when needed. It could monitor and analyze brain activity, on the alert for problematic patterns, just as a cardiac pacemaker sends a jolt of electricity only when it recognizes the heart isn't beating properly. When it detects a problem—say, a tremor or a seizure about to occur—a brain pacemaker could deliver a specially calibrated series of pulses designed to derail that event. Supershrinking electrodes to the size of individual neurons could make placement more precise.

But neurologists need to know more—much more—about brain function. They need to be able to decode brain patterns that signify trouble and those that represent normal activity and to figure out how the many networks interact and overlap.

They're gaining on it. Recently neuroscientists discovered what may be a brain signature for pain: a specific pattern in which neurons fire when people are in intense distress. They found that a specific brain activity correlated perfectly to the amount of subjective pain the patients say they felt. Now the challenge is developing an advanced electrode to listen for these pain signals and send jolts of corrective electricity whenever they appear.

Mayberg is working toward a better understanding of what drives depression and other disorders, using diffusion tensor imaging, to map the brain sections and connective tracts involved with personality, behavior, and diseases (see "Looking Inside Your Brain," p. 71).

But Mayberg and other DBS pioneers are already looking beyond electricity toward biochemistry and newer, less invasive brain modulators. In the future, proteins might be launched to do the job.

Stanford University bioengineer Karl Deisseroth and associates, for instance, are having luck with various methods of stimulating targeted brain areas in mice with light. Proteins called opsins (cousins of retinal cells used in night vision) can be placed noninvasively in the brain and then stimulated with light by a very thin fiber-optic cable rather than electricity from a bulky electrode. In another study, the axons, or long legs of neurons, near the brain's surface were stimulated by light to affect neurons deep in the brain. Deisseroth and others hope to develop these or similar tools to create less invasive switches to modulate brain areas without surgery and more precisely than electrodes.

Meanwhile, studying people with brain implants could help map brain function, identifying areas where electrical stimulation could be most effective or gaining insights into the fundamental structure and function of the brain, such as how your brain coordinates learning a new language or solving an algorithm—or how something as elusive as our subjective experiences can arise from electrical activity in the brain.

CHAPTER SEVEN

Your Bionic Brain
The Merging of Brain with Machines

IN BRIEF

Futurists and science-fiction writers have long speculated about merging human and machine, and especially human brains and computers. These dreams are slowly becoming reality: the deaf are hearing with bionic "ears," the blind see with the aid of electrodes, an amputee is moving a prosthetic arm by thought, and a man paralyzed with locked-in syndrome is "speaking" through a brain electrode connected to a computerized synthesizer. And here's how fast the technology is moving: thought-activated neural implants appeared only in 1996. Just think what will happen in the rest of your lifetime.

Then: Some fiction writers and scientists postulated a time when the brain could be repaired or bettered with bionic parts. But that's all it seemed—fiction—because the technological barriers were formidable.

Now: Advancements in biotechnology and neuroscience are connecting some brains and machines with increasing success in thought-driven technology and replacement of lost neural functions. Some predict we'll also be expanding our memory with microprocessors in our brains within decades.

Tomorrow: Human-machine interconnections will be the norm, with bionic vision, bionic neurons for spinal cord repair, and even bionic memory storage and Internet connection. We'll be able to cure Alzheimer's disease and use thought alone to move machines and pilot spaceships. Some predict we'll even be replaced eventually by our bionic selves: computers with artificial intelligence.

Spare Parts

Artificial parts are old news to humans. We've been making prosthetic replacements such as false teeth, glass eyes, and peg legs for centuries. Now we've got bionic parts living inside the body: knee and hip joint replacements, tooth implants, artificial hearts, breast implants, penile implants, and heart and brain pacemakers.

So why not spare parts for the brain? Although the technologies that make bionic brain implants possible are still in an early stage, in the not-very-distant future they may greatly expand or fix the brain. Neuroimplants of programmable microprocessors may turn parts of your brain into an outsized flash drive, allowing you to carry massive amounts of data inside your head, including your cell phone, your Internet access, a list of everybody's birthdays, your entire family history and contacts (including second cousins once removed), and all your favorite books.

The paralyzed will be able to communicate seamlessly, or even move and walk, thanks to bionic nerve replacement or messages Wi-Fied directly from electrodes implanted on or in the brain. And you won't have to remember where you put those darn keys: a prosthetic hippocampus will eliminate diseases of memory and dementia.

The potential market for neural prostheses just to correct brain ailments alone is enormous. An estimated 5.3 million Americans have Alzheimer's disease; more than 2 million have been paralyzed by spinal cord injuries, amyotrophic lateral sclerosis (ALS), and strokes; more than 1 million are legally blind; and 10 million or more Americans grapple with major depression.

If you're younger than a boomer, the following could happen in your lifetime:

- Bionic eyes will give vision to the blind. Dozens of people worldwide already have implanted artificial retinas, and more than seventy thousand deaf people already are equipped with artificial cochleas—what some call the first true bionic prosthetic.
- Your brain will accept (and incorporate biologically) special microchips to expand memory, contain specific instructions, or act as a portal to download other information. Think of the scene in *The Matrix* where the hero downloads information on how to operate a helicopter from a cell phone into his brain. You could be downloading the entire manual on how to make it.
- Brain-machine interfaces will offer huge opportunities for the able-bodied, such as distant control of machines and virtual touch sensations. We'll be able to run machinery; perform surgery; have virtual sex; or pilot an airplane, ocean liner, or spaceship with thought—or, more correctly, with neural impulses transmitted wirelessly.
- Brain technology will open up life for the paralyzed. Electrodes will "read" neural impulses and transmit them to computers to enable those with no voluntary movement to speak and operate a range of devices from a robot to that spaceship or even a biological avatar to take the brain where your body can't go.
- Nerve regeneration or artificial nerves could return movement to those with spinal cord injuries or debilitating nerve diseases such as ALS or multiple sclerosis within a generation.

WHAT DO YOU MEAN, BIONIC?

The term *bionic* is fairly recent. It describes replacing living biological body parts with engineered artificial parts that are often better than the original. These either revive lost parts or skills or boost human performance. Scientists from several disciplines are working on bionic systems using biological principles.

Most often, the term *bionic* is used to describe an intimate and direct body replacement or supplement, such as in the 1970s TV series *The Six Million Dollar Man*. When former astronaut Steve Austin is severely injured in a plane crash during the opening scenes of the show's pilot, a voice-over tells viewers, reassuringly, not to worry: "We can rebuild him. We have the technology." He has his right arm, both legs, and left eye replaced by lifelike "bionic" implants that give him superhuman strength, speed, and vision.

The 1974 TV series, named for the cost of his operations, is based on a 1972 novel by Martin Caidin, *Cyborg*, another term for merging human with machine. *The Bionic Woman* series (1975) was an offshoot featuring Jaime Sommers, a professional tennis player (and love of Austin) injured in a parachuting accident and given bionic legs, right arm, and ear.

It was science fiction at the time, but today some of these bionic replacements are reality. However, they don't yet have the completely lifelike appearance of those in the TV shows.

- And in the far future, a digital copy of your brain, with memories and emotions intact, could be transferred into a robot, computer, or clone when your present body wears out.

Bionic Brain Research Today

We already have real-life working bionic brain technology of a sort: brain pacemakers based on electrodes in the brain with off-on switches that help people control seizures and tremors. Radio-operated brain implants also exist that can be triggered remotely to provoke some simple processes such as anger (see "Rewiring the Brain Electric," p. 87). Some patients have used neural signals alone to move a cursor on a computer, type messages that can be read or converted through a computerized speech synthesizer, steer a wheelchair, or flex a mechanical arm.

The new bionic brain implants would go way beyond these. Scientists are working toward ways to insert microchips or transmitting electrodes in or on your brain with two major goals. One is for neural implants that would increase your brain's capacity to receive, store, and use information, such as that helicopter manual or a cell phone connection. They foresee neural microprocessors that will be programmed (and reprogrammable remotely) with vast amounts of information, like the ones in your computers, your iPods, and your cameras, but operated solely by your thoughts. The other is for neural implants (either electrodes or microprocessors) that would send thoughts wirelessly out to others, to a prosthetic limb, to computers, or to the controls of that spaceship.

Neurotechno neuroscientists such as Philip R. Kennedy of Neural Signals, Inc., a research and development company working on assistive technology, say they have no doubt that some of this will come about by midcentury. Kennedy is among the leaders in neuro bionic science and the technology that receives and translates neural activity (thought) from the brain into electrical impulses and sends it to a machine counterpart. He and other researchers are experimenting with various kinds of bionic technologies such as brain implants, nerve regeneration, and external electrodes to translate thoughts into actions. They have worked with those who have no voluntary movement of any kind or very limited muscle movement. Among them are patients with locked-in syndrome, ALS, and other conditions.

Another experimental method, targeted muscle reinnervation, is using the nerves that remain after an arm amputation and amplifying their message with electrodes to allow a person to use a prosthetic arm by simply thinking about it, just as she would her own biological arm. Before this, a person could move a prosthetic with thought, but it was conscious and tedious thought for each individual action and motor of the limb. Only a few amputees have been outfitted with this new process and limb so far, and it has a way to go before it's perfected, but it's a huge step forward.

Researchers are also investigating how to send electrical messages in the other direction as well, providing feedback or kinesthetic awareness that would allow a prosthetic hand to "feel" what it is touching, with lifelike veracity, completely separate from sensory inputs into its biological body. Theoretically a father on a space station could caress the hair of his newborn back on earth with a prosthetic hand and receive lifelike sensations. Virtual and very lifelike distant sex would be a possibility as well.

Almost all of this is still experimental. The questions remain: How far can we go in fashioning replacement parts for the brain and the rest of the nervous system? Will the technology somehow actually enable the brain's roughly 100 billion neurons to embrace and connect with an artificial network of neurons—that is, a computer chip? Will we lose some of our humanity in the process? We're glad you asked.

The Britannica in Your Brain—and More

Futurists and optimistic scientists say we will soon be able to download *War and Peace* directly into our brains as easily as we slip books wirelessly into our digital readers today, or more pragmatically, we'll be able to access the Internet and our daily blogs and copy our entire address books and agendas directly onto brain chips. More darkly, some speculate we might also be able to inscribe information into the memory of someone else who is unconscious of the transfer, such as "Send me ten thousand dollars" or "Attack this building."

This depends on developing microprocessors that can merge biologically with our brains, copying (or neuromorphing) the structure of brain circuits onto a silicon chip to be placed in or on your brain, and in some cases allowing brain cells to grow in and around them. The cochlear implant has already shown we can jack into the

---

Star Trek: The Next Generation

The blind can "see" in the Star Trek universe of 2357 or so. Geordi La Forge, who was blind from birth, wears a VISOR (visual instrument and sensory organ replacement) device that scans the electromagnetic spectrum and transmits visual input to the optic nerves from small jacks implanted in his temples. Geordi doesn't have normal human vision, but he can perceive infrared and so can see vital signs such as heart rate and body temperature.

---

brain, and more is on the lab bench. Arrays of electrodes that serve as artificial retinas have been implanted in dozens worldwide.

But scientists don't understand exactly yet how our brain cells take in, process, and relay data. Researchers have many differing theories to explain how the billions of neurons and trillions of synapses that connect them in your head can ping meaningful messages to one another. The oldest idea is that a neural code corresponds to the rate of firing of the voltage spikes in the tiny electrical charges generated by a neuron. More recent work has focused on the precise timing of the intervals between each spike (temporal codes) and the constantly changing patterns of how neurons fire together (population codes).

To download information directly to your brain, they'll need to figure out how to help the neurons recognize, for example, the neural code for the sentence "See Spot run," let alone an entire technical manual. The Defense Advanced Research Projects Agency (DARPA) is interested in something immediate and practical, such as being able to download information for flying a fighter jet.

Artificial Retinas: Giving Sight to the Blind

Researchers have been working for decades toward artificial retinas, and today experimental surgery is giving useful vision to dozens of people worldwide. The procedure works for those with retinitis pigmentosa and macular degeneration—diseases that have destroyed the light-sensing cells (photoreceptors, or rods and cones) in the multilayered retinal membrane at the rear of the eye—who still have optic nerve receptors.

An array of tiny microelectrodes is surgically implanted on the retina. The person wears eyeglasses equipped with a miniature camera, which wirelessly sends images and information to a microprocessor (worn on a belt) that converts the data to an electronic signal and transmits it to a receiver on the eye. This sends signals through a thin cable to the microelectrode array, stimulating it to emit pulses that travel to the optic nerve and, ultimately, to the brain, which perceives patterns of light and dark spots corresponding to the electrodes stimulated, according to researchers. Those using the equipment learn to interpret and translate the patterns intro meaningful images. In the future, such arrays might be tweaked to boost vision in sighted humans, giving us night vision or even the supersight of *The Six Million Dollar Man*.

The project is the result of collaborations among technologies and sciences, from neurology to microelectronics, photovoltaics, and bioengineering; several academic centers worldwide; government researchers, including the National Eye Institute and the Department of Energy's Office of Science; and the corporate research firm Second Sight, which receives substantial government support.

Researchers say the project has spawned even more technologies connecting microelectronics and feedback mechanisms with living tissue. The Department of Energy is saying that such interfaces of living (biotic) neurons with nonliving (abiotic) machines could be adapted for interfaces with other cell types such as those of plants and bacteria.

An Artificial Hippocampus?

Some help toward downloading to the brain might come from the endeavor to build an artificial hippocampus to help people with memory deficits. The hippocampus, seated deep within the brain's temporal lobe, is often damaged in a stroke or by Alzheimer's disease. The project, funded by the National Science Foundation and DARPA, is working toward electronically bypassing a damaged hippocampus to restore the ability to create new memories. Theodore W. Berger at the University of South Carolina and others are studying the way living neurons in the hippocampus communicate, with the goal of developing a computer chip and artificial hippocampus. One study has shown that an artificial hippocampus took over from the biological organ to consolidate memory in a rat.

An artificial hippocampus, however, could present some problems, Gary Stix wrote recently in *Scientific American*. Would an implant overwrite existing memories? Would the neural code for the sentence "See Spot run" be the same for me as it is for you or, for that matter, a native Kurdish speaker? Would the imported memory merge cleanly with other circuitry that provides the context for a sentence—or would "See Spot run" be misinterpreted as a laundry mishap instead of a trotting dog, he posits?

Jacking text into the brain also requires the consideration of inserting electrodes directly into tissue. So far that's been a neurosurgery reserved for the disabled or those with disabling conditions such as epilepsy or Parkinson's disease (see "Rewiring the Brain Electric," p. 87). True, we've been able to detect a brain's electrical activity without

---

Total Recall

This 1990 film, based on a novel by Philip K. Dick, shows what might go wrong when memory implants and existing memories conflict. In 2084, Douglas Quaid is haunted by a recurring dream about Mars. Hoping to find out more, he buys a holiday at Rekall, Inc., which sells implanted memories. But something goes wrong with the memory implantation: he remembers being a secret agent fighting against an evil Mars administrator and goes back to Mars to save the day.

cracking bone for more than a century. Signals from a paralyzed patient can be picked up from what looks like a swimming cap studded with electrodes and transmitted to a computer, where mental impulses can direct typing of letters on a screen or actual surfing of the Web. But the neural technology and the huge amounts of data being considered would require much more precision than we could probably achieve with a wired cap.

Putting Thoughts into Action

Thought-driven devices are today's crème de la crème of brain science. They listen to the brain's instructions for movement, even when actual movement is no longer possible, and decode the signals for use in operating a computer or moving a robot or an artificial limb. The technology for the basic requirements—the powerful microprocessors, improved filters, and longer-lasting and smaller batteries—has advanced rapidly, boosted by funds from many sources, including the U.S. Department of Defense, which sponsors research in prosthetics for wounded war veterans. Years of animal research have revealed neuron activity and the brain's amazing plasticity: the ability to revise itself.

But the research application has been slow. Scientists first had to determine what parts of the brain were controlling movement so they could figure out where to apply the brain wave sensors or electrodes. It's quite complex. Several approaches have been taken, involving tapping into various places in the brain involved with the interface between muscle movement and thought.

One of the ongoing experiments with implanted electrodes could possibly lead to the level of targeting needed. Philip R. Kennedy of Neural Signals, Inc., and his colleagues designed a device that records the output of neurons. The hookup lets a stroke victim send a signal, through thought alone, to a computer that interprets it as, say, a vowel, which can then be vocalized by a speech synthesizer, a step toward forming whole words.

This type of brain-machine interface is more precise than the signals that move a computer cursor over letters of the alphabet to spell out words or operate an on-off switch. It's tapping directly into the section of the brain responsible for speech. While Kennedy's volunteers will also communicate with speech synthesized by a computer because they no longer can move vocal muscles, their speech is created directly through thought to vocal nerves, to muscles, to computer, a huge difference in magnitude of difficulty and in effect. It also opens the door for many other uses.

"Thought is gazillions of neurons firing in ensembles," says Kennedy. "We're trying to pick the right ones, and there's an enormous amount of trial and error." He compares thought to a wind blowing over a vast field of wheat and his work as looking for the specific stalks of wheat that move. He has had to find a way to separate speech signals from neural noise without animal research to guide him, because no other animal except humans has speech.

Brown University neuroscientist John Donoghue, the second scientist after Kennedy to develop a neural prosthesis for human implantation, is teaming up with biomedical engineer Hunter Peckham of Case Western Reserve University, who has developed an electrical device that stimulates nerves or muscles to enable some movement after a partial or lower-level spinal cord injury. Peckham has a system that allows simple, preprogrammed motions, such as boosting a person from a wheelchair to a walker. By linking a neural prosthesis to the device, Donoghue and Peckham hope to create an enormously more effective system.

Tapping into individual neurons is next: using nanoscale fibers, measuring 100 nanometers or less in diameter, that could easily tap into single neurons because of their dimensions and their electrical and mechanical properties. Jun Li of Kansas State University and his colleagues have crafted a brush-like structure in which nanofiber bristles serve as electrodes for stimulating or receiving neural signals. Li foresees it as a way to stimulate neurons to allay Parkinson's disease or depression or to flex astronauts' muscles during long space flights to prevent the inevitable muscle wasting that occurs in zero gravity.

A.I. Artificial Intelligence

This 2001 Spielberg film could as easily be called "artificial love." Set in the mid-twenty-first century, when advanced humanoid robots are capable of human emotions, *A.I.* features an android child programmed to love and a sexbot called Gigolo Joe programmed as a male prostitute and played (very appealingly) by Jude Law. At least one scientist thinks robot love is not that far off (see "Not Tonight, Dear; I Have to Reboot," p. 113).

Thought-driven technology will change the lives of millions of people, including the many thousands conscious but now entombed within their own bodies in what's called locked-in syndrome, and the thousands of wounded warriors returning from battle with missing limbs and devastating brain injuries. And it could open tremendous opportunities for fully abled people in the future who would like to take their minds where no man's body has gone before—into deepest space or the deepest of ocean depths, for example, through the "senses" of a thought-driven robot.

How and Why Your Brain Is Better Than a Computer—for Now

The enormous progress and promise of brain bionics leads inevitably to even more comparisons between the human brain and its creation, the computer.

For now at least, your brain is better than any computer. But how is that so? How does the brain, which transmits chemical signals between neurons in a relatively sluggish thousandth of a second, end up performing some tasks faster and more efficiently than the most powerful digital processors? The secret appears to reside in how the brain organizes its slow-acting electrical components. The brain does not execute coded instructions; instead, it activates links, or synapses, between neurons. Each such activation is equivalent to executing a

NOT TONIGHT, DEAR; I HAVE TO REBOOT

A brain-machine interface could become even more intimate, projects artificial intelligence researcher David Levy. He proposes, and seriously, that some of us may find love and happiness by marrying robots in the not-too-distant future.

The Internet has already made it possible to fall in love and agree to marry without ever having met face to face, he says. And because research shows that those with strong social networks and relationships live longer and are happier, "If the alternative is that you are lonely and sad and miserable, is it not better to find a robot that claims to love you and acts like it loves you?" he asks.

Science-fiction fans have witnessed plenty of action between humans and artificial life-forms in books, TV, and films. And the interactions between humans and robots have become increasingly personal. Robots initially found work in factories (where most are still employed) but have moved into your home as computerized interactive games and in the form of digital pets such as Tamagotchis and the Sony Aibo. And people often personalize and name their machines.

So why not let them into your heart and bed? Levy, the author of "Love and Sex with Robots," has been exploring the way humans interact with computers, a topic for which he earned his doctorate from the University of Maastricht in the Netherlands.

Although a humanoid robot who looks and acts like the sexbot Gigolo Joe, played by Jude Law in the film *A.I.,* is still a long way off, computers with personalities are already here and can be programmed to interact.

For the sake of good taste, we'll avoid discussion of life-size dolls. But Levy does not: "It's just a matter of time before someone takes parts from a vibrator, puts them into a doll, and maybe adds some basic speech electronics, and then you'll have a fairly primitive sex robot," he says.

Massachusetts, he predicts, will be the first U.S. state to legalize marriage with robots. By the way, he's married to a human (who doesn't share all of his beliefs).

digital instruction, so one can compare how many connections a brain activates every second with the number of instructions a computer executes during the same time.

Synaptic activity is staggering: 10 quadrillion neural connections a second! It would take 1 million Intel Pentium-powered computers to match that rate, plus a few hundred megawatts to juice them up.

One small, innovative community of engineers is making significant progress in copying neuronal organization and function. Researchers speak of having "morphed" the structure of neural connections into silicon circuits, creating neuromorphic microchips. If successful, this work could lead to implantable silicon retinas for the blind and sound processors for the deaf that last for thirty years on a single nine-volt battery. The technological obstacles are significant but so fascinating (and potentially fruitful) that they are enough to keep a cross-section of scientists working toward solutions.

What's Next? And What About My Brain?

The excitement over the bionic possibilities of our brains obscures our lack of knowledge of the underlying mechanisms, not to mention the technical hurdles.

Among the challenges are finding (or making) biologically compatible and very long-lasting materials for the implants, lowering the power levels need to run them, and finding biological sources for that power. Some materials would need to be biodegradable or able to be absorbed by the body when the function is no longer needed. And forget computer analogies. The challenge in figuring out how to move information into the brain—the task of forming the multitude of connections that make a memory—is vastly different from magnetizing a set of bits on a hard disk. Complex information like the contents of a book would require the interactions of a very large number of brain cells over a very large area of the nervous system, observes one neuroscientist.

But oh—consider the potential, from the prosaic to the grand. Jacking into the brain could enable those with no voluntary movement to move, speak, and work—and give extra-human powers to others. A neurochip and computer backpack might allow a person to move limbs that have been stilled by spinal injury. The rest of us would just like to be able to download traveler's Japanese for that trip to Tokyo.

Your tax dollars are supporting some of this research through National Institutes of Health funding or defense department spending. DARPA has invested millions in brain-machine interface research, from mind-controlled prosthetics to neural chips to technology for digitally capturing everything a person sees or does.

NASA is interested too. The possibility of controlling external devices using brain-machine connections could have a tremendous impact on the endangered future of the space program. Such technology could replace humans with robots for dangerous space walks and allow faster and better control of the complex machinery, especially in weightless situations where pushing buttons is difficult.

Kaiser Permanente, the health maintenance organization, is already offering members a free flash drive with recent medical records. Implanting a neural chip programmed with those records, and with your past actions, thoughts, and memories, is next. We already have implanted identification chips for pets, wildlife, and humans.

John Donoghue predicts that in the next five years, brain-machine interfaces will let a paralyzed person pick up a cup and take a drink of water, and that in some distant future, these systems might be refined so that a person with an upper spinal cord injury might accomplish what is now impossible—perhaps even playing a game of basketball with prosthetics that would make a reality of *The Six Million Dollar Man*. An understanding of central nervous system development may let educators discover the best ways to teach children and determine at what point (and for which child) certain teaching techniques or material would work best to allow them to acquire certain capabilities in the shortest possible time.

Some ask if this means that humans will become machines. It's actually more of a question of how much of our human brain and body will become like machines (or computers), say experts. Your brain is well on its way to a machine interface—psychologically at least. If you were born after 1980, you are accustomed to being hooked into electronic gadgets with a near constant stream of information.

Some extreme futurists project that we are on our way to making ourselves obsolete. They say the thing that makes us most human, our brain, may be upstaged by our creation, the computer. Computer scientist Ray Kurzweil has in fact posited that humans will eventually achieve a form of immortality by transferring a digital blueprint of their brains into computers or robots. In the most extreme of projections, Kurzweil predicts we could have cyborgs among us by midcentury or maybe the century's end. These machine-human hybrids could be the beginning of the end of us as masters of the universe, as our computerized creations take over and keep us as, perhaps, a curiosity and an endangered species.

There's also the dream of eternity as a brain grafted (or copied-and-pasted) into the latest humanoid bot—the wholesale transfer of "self" into a machine-based facsimile.

The 2009 science fiction film *Avatar* explores another possibility: a biological extension for your brain in a clone (or avatar) that can be controlled wirelessly by your thoughts and send back sensory information—in effect, taking your consciousness where you can't (or don't want to) take your actual brain and body, such as an alien planet.

Although cloning humans is—for now—forbidden, it's possible. So is wireless mind control of such a living avatar: We're already able to control robots and computers wirelessly with neural impulses, and animals with brain implants.

A lot of research and technology has to happen before the seamless and apparently device-free mind-meld portrayed in *Avatar* could be a reality. It's still a distant dream (or nightmare). But one day, your brain may benefit from bionic or biologic spare parts or even clones to help overcome many of the injuries and disabilities of mind and body.

CHAPTER EIGHT

The Possible Dreams

Stem Cells, Gene Therapy, and Nanotechnology

IN BRIEF

Brain surgery may soon be a thing of the past, reserved for the most desperate cases. Technology and science are finding ways to get inside human heads without cutting them open, to diagnose and treat everything from schizophrenia to stroke and brain tumors. Some of these—stem cell research and gene replacement therapy—have been in the works for decades and are showing new promise after years of near misses and controversy. But one—nanomedicine—is brand new, the fruit of startling new research into the very, very small.

Then: As far back as 7,000 B.C., most brain injuries were fixed by doing nothing or by cutting into the skull and parts of the brain.

NOW: Noninvasive treatments are preferred, but tumors, Parkinson's disease, epilepsy and other movement disorders, and even depression are treated with neurosurgery from major skull openings to implants of thin electrodes.

Tomorrow: Surgery will be rare. We'll send drugs, chemicals, and tiny surgical instruments into the brain through nanotechnology; replace defective genes or cells with ease; or even clone an exact replica of your brain or brain cells.

In the 1966 film *Fantastic Voyage*, a brilliant scientist is in a coma with a brain clot from an attempted assassination. To save his life, a submarine and its crew (which includes sixties' sex symbol Raquel Welch) are temporarily shrunk to one micrometer in size and injected into his bloodstream. They have one hour to swim to the clot, repair it, and escape before they begin to revert to normal size and are recognized and destroyed by the injured scientist's immune system. After many adventures throughout the body, the crew destroys the clot and escapes in a teardrop just in time.

This is not, as it turns out, science fiction any longer. Oh, the parts about the submarine and mini-humans and floating out on a teardrop are—but not the concept. In the not-too-distant future, minuscule nanorobots may indeed swim through the bloodstream to the site of a blood clot or other injury and make a repair.

Amazing as this is, other nanotechnology in the works is even more brain boggling, such as preparing specialized protein molecules that swim to a predetermined site and are activated externally by probes or lasers that turn off or on specific genes. Talk about special delivery. To researchers, this is even sexier than Raquel Welch.

But wait! It gets better. That scientist could also be healed by gene replacement or stem cell therapies—two other ways of getting inside to fix the brain without opening the skull. These three very promising therapies and treatment modes are being heavily investigated and

BLOOD WILL TELL: YOUR INNER HIGHWAY

Because blood bathes every organ in your body, it's an excellent way to examine the health of your entire body system, including your brain. Emerging technology can measure minuscule amounts of blood or even single cells, forge a diagnosis and a treatment plan, and then perhaps use the bloodstream to deliver it.

We might soon be able to see an imbalance in proteins or messenger RNA that could reveal a disease and pinpoint its location and even its subtype. One could tell, for example, if a person has a brain tumor, what type and subtype it is, and its stage, and suggest which gene-focused treatments might be most effective—without ever opening the skull. And doctors may be able to use your blood highway to treat it noninvasively as well.

Researchers have been able to track prion disease (a fatal brain disease also called mad cow disease) injected into mice. Using specialized software that manipulated 30 million measurements, they analyzed messenger RNA from mouse brains and identified factors that predicted prion disease before there were any symptoms. The next step is creating nanoparticles to deliver potent drugs only to a specific diseased area such as a brain tumor.

Such measures could not always guarantee a cure, but they might someday be able to make often-fatal diseases such as cancer and AIDS manageable with medications, much as diabetes is now.

might in fact eventually work together. Gene therapy alters or replaces defective or missing genes; stem cell therapies coax replacement cells to take the form and function of defective or missing cells; and nanotechnology, the science of the very, very small, is working on ways to send treatments into the brain through the bloodstream. How small? A micrometer is one-millionth of a meter; a nanometer is one *billionth* of a meter, too small to be seen by an ordinary microscope.

Research on gene therapy and stem cells is overlapping in many areas, as the biomedical research has many similar therapeutic goals. Both have been used to treat severe combined immune deficiency (also called the "Bubble Boy" disease), a rare condition. Stem cells could also be used to deliver genes to the desired spot, and nanotechnology may work in concert with these therapies.

Nanomedicine may be a new term to many people, but both gene and stem cell research have been in the news so much and been the objects of so much hope it's hard to believe they have been under study for only a few decades. There have been many troubles and setbacks getting them under way. Granted, there are huge technological and scientific obstacles, but major roadblocks have been ethical and moral controversies, ranging from legal and other objections to using stem cells derived from discarded human embryos to the dangers of implanting genes in humans to the cloning of cells (or whole humans).

The research has spawned vigorous and at times violent discussion about the human rights of human embryos. There is as well an entire industry of services, including one in which parents pay thousands to have stem cells from the umbilical cord blood of their newborns extracted and stored as insurance for future medical needs when stem cell therapies are available.

The Future of Stem Cells

It's easy to forget that human embryonic stem cell research has been around only since 1998, when scientists first identified and isolated stem cells from human embryos. The discovery offered great potential for the body, especially the brain, to self-renew biologically.

There are many different kinds of stem cells, but all have the ability to divide and create exact copies of themselves, which then go on indefinitely. These can develop into cells for specific tissues and organs, therefore (theoretically) replacing dead or damaged cells just about anywhere in the body. The basic types are the embryonic or pluripotent stem cells, which can develop into just about any kind of cell in the body, and the tissue-specific stem cells (or adult stem cells), which have already chosen what they will become. Neural stem cells become various types of brain cells but cannot become other tissues.

Transplanted into a human, these cells could replace diseased, dead, or damaged tissue, including neurons damaged by anything from trauma to disease.

Repair of spinal cord injury has been a holy grail of stem cell research, and there has been some success. In 2005, scientists showed that they could make paralyzed rats walk again by injecting cells into the spinal cord within seven days after the injury. And in January 2009, the FDA approved the first clinical trial to test a stem cell–based treatment for spinal cord injury in humans.

But so far only one stem cell therapy has been approved in humans: bone marrow transplants, in which a sick person's immune system is destroyed and then rebuilt by cells transplanted from a donor's bone marrow into the patient. The process is risky—the recipient must be isolated from any possibility of infectious disease until the new immune system boots up—but it has been successful for thousands.

Research centers around the world are investing billions in working toward viable stem cell therapies. A major stem cell initiative is under way at the California Institute for Regenerative Medicine (CIRM) in San Francisco, which has $3 billion in California funding to support research at the state's universities and research institutions. The institute reports that researchers are successfully transplanting stem cells into animals with neurodegenerative diseases. In mice they've corrected the abnormal gait of Parkinson's disease, improved memory loss from an Alzheimer's disease–like condition, and eliminated the jerky body movements of Huntington's disease. A half-dozen children with advanced cases of a fatal neurodegenerative disease called neuronal ceroid ipofuscinosis, or Batten disease, are being followed in a clinical trial, with some early success. The major challenges to treatment are getting enough of the right kinds of cells, getting them into the right place in the brain, and controlling the cells so they don't mutate or start a runaway process that could produce cancer. Rejection is also a possibility with some stem cell transplants.

FIXING STROKES WITH STEM CELLS

Injecting stem cells into the brains of mice that recently suffered a stroke can reduce damage to neurons by up to 60 percent, according to new research. But the stem cells do not simply replace damaged nerve cells as previously believed. Instead they affect the brain's immune cells, called *microglia*, which go into overdrive during stroke, attacking and destroying healthy tissues. In the mouse experiment, the stem cells calmed down the microglia and got them to call off their assault. The treated mice performed better than their untreated peers on a battery of movement, cognitive, and behavioral tests.

Retinal Stem Cells from Adults Show Promise

Stem cells do exist in adults. In fact, we have neural stem cells that retain the ability to become other types of brain cells and could serve as possible treatments for ailments ranging from vision impairment to Parkinson's disease to spinal cord injuries. However, these arise in the hippocampus, buried deep within the brain, and researchers are understandably reluctant to go digging around for them, Sally Temple, founder of the New York Neural Stem Cell Institute, said at the 2009 World Stem Cell Summit.

But Temple and her team have discovered other, more accessible neural stem cell candidates in the retinal pigment epithelium (RPE), a layer of tissue at the base of the retina that comes into being within thirty to fifty days of conception, before many other parts of the neural system differentiate. Cells from this area of the eye can be easily harvested from retinal fluid that is usually discarded during retinal surgery, she explained, and they don't have to be taken from embryos.

After culturing RPE cells, her group was able to coax them into showing potential to become a host of different visual and other neural cells. The researchers also found, to their surprise, that in working with donated cadaver eyes, cells harvested from ninety-nine-year-old eyes had just as much plasticity as those from twenty-two-year-old eyes. They are similarly flexible because they have been "held in a dormant state," she said.

Other researchers are looking for the perfect stem cells that could become photoreceptor cells, and there are advances in gene therapy for vision disorders as well. In the future, combined therapies might work best. However, even if stem cell research continues to show progress for improving vision or other neural disorders, a usable treatment could still be years, and likely decades, away. Meanwhile, an artificial retina is helping many.

The Promise of Gene Therapy

In the 1990s, gene therapy was hailed as an impending revolution in medicine because of its potential to attack disease at its genetic roots: to literally fix a broken gene.

In gene therapy, a functional and healthy gene replaces one that is dead, sick, or mutated or provides new genetic instructions to fight a disease or condition. The new gene is transported into the patient's cells through a vector, such as a weakened or inactive virus. It may not involve replacing the gene directly, but rather replacing a gene to make a protein or other chemical needed for optimal brain function.

The early research results did not live up to the hype, however, and over the past decade, gene therapy has taken some hard hits. Much hope was destroyed in 1999 when an eighteen-year-old patient suffered an unexpectedly severe immune reaction and died during an experiment. Gene therapy also left three others with leukemia. In 2008, it was tied to the death of a thirty-six-year-old Illinois woman undergoing treatment for rheumatoid arthritis, although further investigation cleared her therapy of the blame.

Gene therapy products are still being studied in a wide variety of diseases, including cancer, genetic diseases, and HIV/AIDS. Although there are currently no FDA-approved gene therapy products for use in the United States, there's optimism with the more than eight

A GENETICS REFRESHER

Every cell in the human body carries a full copy of the human genome, which is made up of three billion pairs of DNA bases, the letters of the genetic alphabet. Those "letters" encode some twenty-five thousand genes, representing instructions for operating cells and tissues.

Inside each cell, genes are transcribed into a more portable form: discrete snippets of messenger RNA, so-called because it carries those instructions into cells that read the RNA and churn out chains of amino acids according to the instructions. Those amino acid chains, in turn, fold themselves into proteins, the three-dimensional molecular machines that execute most of the functions of life.

In a biological system—you—all of these "data" are transmitted, processed, integrated, and ultimately executed through networks of proteins interacting with one another and with other molecules inside the cells. Disease is the result of something perturbing the network's normal programming. It could be a flaw in the system, such as a random change in DNA that alters an encoded instruction, or some environmental influence that causes change from outside. That could be ultraviolet radiation that causes DNA damage that eventually leads to melanoma, for example.

Your emotions can also affect your genes, turning on an inactive gene for a disease by an emotional or traumatic experience. Research in animals has shown that bullying or other abuse that creates stress can affect gene expression. So the genetic basis of disease doesn't just mean what you inherit, because some of the inherited genetic factors remain dormant or recessive and may never come into play in a way that directly affects your life. It's the genes that are activated—those that are triggered and *expressed* in sci talk—that determine your health and, it seems, your happiness.

hundred ongoing trials. A dozen cancer treatments and a heart treatment are in the last phase of clinical trials. Doctors have announced promising results from an early-phase trial for Parkinson's disease. A therapy that has restored sight to seventy congenitally blind dogs is being tested in humans at the University of Pennsylvania, and eight research groups are gearing up to test new HIV treatments. China has approved two cancer treatments, but their efficacy remains unclear. Reports from Europe and Japan say gene therapy has helped some patients with Parkinson's disease. In a case reported from Jichi Medical University in Japan in 2009, five of six patients improved motor function after having a dopamine-producing enzyme stored in a virus and injected into their brains.

Today most gene therapy studies are aimed at cancer and hereditary genetic diseases such as some of the worst neural diseases, including Huntington's, Parkinson's, and amyotrophic lateral sclerosis. Scientists know the single genes responsible for these. But they are finding that many, and perhaps most, neurological and even psychological diseases involve many genes. It has been very difficult to track the genetic and epigenetic basis of schizophrenia, Alzheimer's disease, and even chronic depression, because these seem to involve many genes. So there's no telling how long it may take to develop effective gene therapies for most brain conditions.

Nanomedicine

Nanomedicine has been around for about a decade, although it was conceived of more than a half-century ago—by a physicist.

It's one of the new polygamous marriages of medicine, engineering, and physics that may change the way many diseases are treated. Nanotechnology is the engineering of functional systems at the molecular scale. That could involve developing technology to send molecules of protein, medications, or other materials into the brain to make repairs and to turn neurons or genes off and on to stop seizures, tremors, and depression.

And that includes creating tiny nano engines or robot "machines" as well as biological systems, a complex subject that rapidly gets much too complicated for our purposes here. Remember that a nano is one-billionth of a meter, and at that scale, some unique and remarkable physical properties apply.

In medicine, nanotechnology can be used for instruments as well as for methods to deliver medication. Much like in gene therapy, cancer cells or genes could be precisely targeted. Nanoparticles would take just about any material that can be captured and encapsulated (or packaged), such as genetic materials, vaccines, and drugs, and deliver them to the selected spot.

The nano delivery vans include simple lipid shells (liposomes— tiny spheres made of the same material as a cell membrane) that passively leak through tumor blood vessel walls, then slowly release a traditional chemotherapy drug into the tissue. Newer nanoparticles are complex and include exterior elements such as antibodies to target tumor-specific proteins and materials that minimize the particles' interaction with healthy tissues.

It shows tremendous promise for treating brain tumors without surgery and without the chemotherapy or radiation therapies that also injure healthy tissue. Because nanoparticles are smaller than cells but larger than molecules, they could carry a payload of molecules designed to bind with specific proteins and thus deliver drugs just where they are needed.

LEAPING THE BLOOD-BRAIN BARRIER

Delivering drugs across the blood-brain barrier is one of the most promising applications of nanotechnology for treating brain disease. Your brain has a defense against intruders: it's the blood-brain barrier that keeps most materials in circulating blood, including bacteria, from entering the brain. It keeps the bloodstream separate from the cerebral spinal fluid, a clear liquid that bathes and cushions part of the brain. The blood-brain barrier does allow some molecules, proteins, and chemicals to cross the barrier (barbiturate drugs, for example). The challenge for scientists has been how to deliver medication across that fence to parts of an ailing brain, while keeping other substances out. Nanomedicine may provide that method.

In a human cancer trial, a chemotherapy drug inside a nanoparticle that was designed to accumulate in tumors was effective in some of the people with advanced cancers: the targeted tumor shrank considerably. In a recent study, researchers sent nanoparticles stocked with gold fragments to tumors in mice, then applied low-level heat that raised the temperature of the metal slightly to destroy the tumor but not healthy surrounding tissue.

Such small and precise payloads also mean less chemotherapy or other toxic drugs and fewer adverse side effects. In fact, after acute cancer therapy, teeny amounts of these drugs could be administered via nanoparticles on a maintenance basis rather than waiting to see if a cancer returns.

Nanoparticles may also be used to help deliver stem cells to the right address or to enhance their action. Recent mouse research at MIT used the dual therapy to carry the gene for vascular endothelial growth factor to stimulate regeneration of damaged blood vessel tissue.

The National Nanotechnology Initiative 2010 budget provides $1.6 billion for medical and other research and applications. As greater understanding of the molecular transitions from health to disease and vice versa is gained, the nanoparticle approach is likely to play an increasing role in the treatment of disease at the molecular level.

What's Next? And What About My Brain?

There's much to hope for in the therapies explored in this chapter. The most dreaded hereditary neurological diseases could be cured by gene replacement or stem cells, and damage from stoke, the third leading cause of death and a major crippler, could be mitigated by stem cells before the worst of the damage is done—or the damage could be prevented or fixed through nanotechnology. Stem cells or gene replacement might fix brains damaged by many causes, including Alzheimer's disease.

Moreover, in the future we might be able to determine many aspects of our health with a portable pinprick test with instant results, similar to that available to people with diabetes to test their blood sugar. The extreme (really extreme) miniaturization of technologies possible in nanomedicine could make diagnostic measurements possible with the teeniest drop of blood or even single cells, predict the nanotechnology experts, and the cost could eventually be mere pennies per test.

These technologies will also lead to viewing the body as a system of interacting molecular networks rather than individual parts, much as new brain research recognizes the brain as a widespread system of interrelating circuits. These and other advances will lead to more understanding about the systemic and molecular basis of disease and, from that, ways to cure it. Experts are moving toward creating a therapeutic system that could carry drugs, each with its own customized release rate, to specific parts of the brain. When this system is used to deliver chemotherapy to parts of the body, your brain could be spared the fuzzy thinking and other cognitive damage of side effects called chemobrain.

Cloning—the process of making an exact DNA duplicate of another organism, organ, or cell—could become a reality scientifically, as well as ethically and legally. Cloning cells or organs could at the very least help millions and could be within reach. In fact, stem cells actually "clone" themselves as they reproduce. Cloning whole organisms, as in the film *Avatar* or your dearly departed dog or deceased mate or your own brain, is something else. There have been claims of cloning human and animal embryos, and services to clone pets are offered for quite a bit of money. But there are concerns: remember Dolly the sheep? She died at a young age amid speculation that the older DNA in her cloning made her age prematurely.

Given the uproar over ethics, whole human (or whole brain) cloning is unlikely to happen in your lifetime. But who knows? Given the breakneck pace of research and the financial incentives, the future is a vast unknown.

CHAPTER NINE

Neuroethics

Facing the Dark Side

IN BRIEF

The study of neuroethics emerged in the 1960s—and just in time, some say. Although the future of much of neuroscience is still unknown, one thing is mind-numbingly certain: its remarkable applications are going to keep lots of lawyers, courts, philosophers, and ethicists busy for a long time to come. The questions and issues the new sciences raise concern fairness, civil rights, privacy, morality, and even the very essence of what it is to be human. We would seem to be headed for some interesting times—and litigation.

Then: New medical treatments and technologies brought troublesome ethical questions: Who should get the rare herb, vaccine, surgery, or organ for transplantation or be first in line for life-saving emergency medicine? There were few safeguards for those in clinical trials, little guarantee of confidentiality, and not much litigation.

NOW: Neuroethics is just one of the many fields concerned with ethical issues in medicine: abortion; use of embryonic stem cells; genetic testing; and neuroimaging to predict brain disease, criminal tendencies, or mental defects. And lawsuits—Should they be called neurolitigation?—are driving many concerns.

Tomorrow: The avalanche of brain knowledge and accompanying technology is opening issues and raising ethical questions never before encountered that go to the core of constitutional rights and the options for therapies for brain health in ways never before imagined.

There's no doubt that the expansion of neuroscience and neuro-technology is bringing phenomenal potential benefits for all of us, along with thorny questions about their ethical use.

The issues are immense, and just about every research university has a major investment in studying them. Among the many organizations examining current and future dilemmas is the MacArthur Foundation. Its $10 million Project on Law and Neuroscience involves some forty neuroscientists, legal specialists, and philosophers looking at questions of criminal responsibility, prediction of criminal behavior, treatment options, and issues of psychopathy and drug addiction and how these affect our understandings of responsibility, punishment, and the use of neuroscience in legal decision making.

The primary issues facing medical ethicists are not totally new. Some of them, in fact, are as old as the human race and hinge squarely on the humane treatment of humans. The powerful have exploited and often injured humans to discover what makes us tick.

Three in the twentieth century were particularly infamous:

- The experiments by Nazi scientists and doctors on those who were considered defective or "undesirables."

- The Tuskegee, Alabama, study that in 1942 recruited 399 impoverished African American sharecroppers with syphilis before there was a treatment. Over the course of the study, effective therapy became available, but scientists withheld it from the subjects in order to continue the study. Some of the original subjects died from the disease.

- Involuntary sterilization of those identified as "mental defectives" and involuntary drastic psychosurgery that continued well into the latter half of the twentieth century. The developer of the frontal lobotomy was awarded a Nobel Prize in 1949.

More recent issues have involved privacy in genetics testing and ownership of your own body parts, blood, tissues, and genes. Fair allocation of new technology continues to be a major issue, and the controversies surrounding the ethical use of gene therapy and the civil and legal rights controversies regarding embryonic stem cells continue.

But advances in neurotechnology have put an extra spin on ethical considerations. Technology that is used to explore and understand the brain can be used to exploit as well. Brain scans, for example, which are showing more and more about how a living brain functions, also offer opportunities to predict and possibly control or change behavior, illness, cognitive performance, intelligence, and even character, not to mention insurance coverage. Indeed, many of the issues reach into constitutional rights, such as privacy, fairness, civil rights, rights to a trial by a jury of one's peers, and equal access to expensive high-tech treatments, says Hank T. Greely, the Deane F. and Kate Edelman Johnson Professor of Law at Stanford University.

The editors of *Scientific American* have been mulling these many questions as far back as 2003, when they asked: What kind of privacy safeguards would be needed if a machine could read your thoughts? Will your thoughts condemn you in court—or worse, as in the movie *Minority Report,* the dark science-fiction story of precogs who predict crime before it occurs and punish the "perpetrator" accordingly?

Will cognition enhancers exacerbate differences between rich and poor? Or will they relegate social diversity to the status of historical artifact? What happens if we deduce through neuroimaging the physiological basis for morality? And, by the way, what happens to free will?

Columnist William Safire popularized the term *neuroethics*. The fledgling field held one of its first conferences in May 2002 at Stanford University to begin to map a strategy to deal with the ethics of neuroscience. The list of moral and social issues attached to neurotechnologies is long enough to position ethicists near the top on lists of hot jobs. But do we really need a new subdiscipline of a subdiscipline? After all, we have bioethics, which already compartmentalizes a larger field that has been around since Aristotle and Hippocrates.

The answer appears to be yes.

Stem Cells: Still Fighting After All These Years

Anyone who thinks that the public debate over embryonic stem cells (ESCs) is nearing an end is in for a rude awakening.

True, it seemed like happy days were here again for the ESC research community after Barack Obama took office in 2009. The U.S. Food and Drug Administration green-lighted an application to pursue the first phase I clinical trial of an ESC-based therapy (for spinal cord injury), and President Obama lifted the burdensome restrictions on federally funded ESC studies imposed by his predecessor in 2001. Laboratories receiving federal money are once again free to work on the cell lines of their choice (with some important restrictions). So scientists at last have mostly what they have been asking for.

But the battle isn't over. In March 2009, ten of eighteen members of former president George W. Bush's Council on Bioethics issued a press release criticizing the Obama administration's policy as unethical. Days after the president's executive order, the Georgia State Senate approved the Ethical Treatment of Human Embryos Act, which would bar the deliberate creation of embryos for ESCs.

And we can expect more of the same. Stem cell research continues to be a pawn in a larger political game being fought over abortion, women's reproductive autonomy, and the tension between individual rights and notions of public morality. So while researchers continue to struggle to overcome the obstacles to effective stem cell therapies, which are at least a decade off, the continuing controversy over this area may be one of the biggest barriers.

Liar, Liar: Can Brain Scans Reveal the Truth?

The ability to tell when someone is lying is of keen interest to most of us, and especially attorneys eager to bring brain scans into courtrooms, law enforcement agents looking for evidence of wrongdoing, and singles wanting to look into the hearts and heads of potential mates.

But few are convinced that today's brain scans are accurate enough to tell the truth, or the whole truth, including the world's foremost lie catcher, Paul Ekman, emeritus professor of psychology and the master of facial expression recognition who is the science behind the TV show *Lie to Me*. To begin with, Ekman says, most studies are poorly designed, because participants have nothing to lose by lying or telling the truth and because even the term *lying* means many different things to people, skewing the premise.

Many experts also agree that the technology is not accurate enough. Today's brain scans can show where your brain is activated by whatever your mind and body are doing and feeling, but not necessarily what that means or even if you are lying about telling a lie. So your amygdala lights up. What does that mean in definable terms? (see "The Limits of Brain Scans," p. 79).

No lie detection method is 100 percent accurate so far. Greely and Judy Illes, now at the University of British Columbia, coauthored a major article in 2007 in the *American Journal of Law and Medicine* that explored the problems and lacks of MRI research, and found that lie detection studies conducted to that point had failed to prove that fMRI is as "effective as a lie detector in the real world at *any* accuracy

Minority Report

In this 2002 film, there's not much murder in Washington, D.C., in the year 2054, thanks to the specialized Precrime Police Department, which identifies and arrests potential criminals before they act based on fore-knowledge provided by three psychics. But when the head of the Precrime Department (played by Tom Cruise) is fingered wrongly as a potential murderer, the system is shown to be flawed and begins to unravel. Could a similar precrime department arise based on brain scans that show ten-dencies to violence?

level." Thousands of articles have been published on MRI research every year since then, and most haven't gone very far toward changing that assessment.

Moreover, it could be possible to fool a brain scan: people could skew the procedure by thinking strongly of the "truth" or emotion they want "read" by the fMRI. Actors, sociopaths, and others skilled at presenting differing personas could manipulate brain scans as well.

Responsibility: My Sick Brain Made Me Do It (The Devil Made Me Do It?)

Contrary to what you read and hear, brain scans have not (yet, at this writing) been admissible in any U.S. court. And many legal experts hope they won't be until many issues have been clarified, mainly those about the accuracy of such scans to depict thoughts and emotions. And since brain scans show that the brains of psychopaths and those prone to violence are different from those of other people, will these scans be used to arrest and jail potential criminals before they act, as in the film *Minority Report,* in which psychics identify crimes before they happen? Would scanning your brain be illegal search and seizure, a violation of the Fourth Amendment, or self-incrimination, the Fifth Amendment?

THE BUSINESS OF BRAIN SCANS

Meanwhile, entrepreneurs have discovered how to make a buck on brain scans. There's the company named Brain Fingerprinting—also the name of a controversial technique that claims to tell whether specific information is stored in someone's brain by using an EEG (electroencephalograph) to measure brainwave responses to words, phrases, or pictures. Its inventor claims the brain's processing of known information, such as the details of a crime stored in the brain, is revealed by a specific pattern in the EEG. Although a clutch of studies (conducted by the founder of the business) claim a high level of accuracy for the technique, scientists and lawyers remain skeptical. Testimony was allowed in a murder case in India in 2008, when two life sentences were handed out based on technology called brain electrical oscillation signature profiling, something similar to an EEG.

But it has been overshadowed by the sexier and more accurate MRI and fMRI scans, being offered freelance by businesses such as the No Lie MRI Company (yes, that is the actual name) and Cephos. In fact, Cephos (for a while at least) was offering free brain scans to those who would try to use them in court cases.

MRIs are being used in courts in the sentencing phase of criminal trials, mainly to show that brain damage or abnormalities may have prevented a defendant from forming intent to commit the crime. And that brings up another issue: if a brain has been damaged, can its owner be held responsible for his or her actions—theft, addictions, pedophilia, murder? Does a damaged brain mean its owner doesn't have free will? If so, what happens to our criminal system?

Greely and other experts in neuroethics and the law believe brain scans will have less overall impact there than some think. "You may not have free will," he concedes, "but locking up an offender spares others." He does think there will be some changes in individual cases where a defendant does not have the capacity to control actions, but primarily in sentencing. Time will tell.

Criminal court isn't the only legal venue for scans. There's also a future in disability claims and civil cases. Every year hundreds of thousands of claims and charges about pain and suffering go to court in disability, worker compensation, and civil suits. If there is no clear-cut physical evidence, the person suing for damages related to pain has often had to rely on his or her own persuasive testimony to get a settlement, and judges and juries have had to try to discover the truth. All too often, a claimant is exaggerating or out-and-out lying. Pain is, after all, subjective: it exists in the brain. If an MRI can show a person is in pain—and how much pain—or not, that could tip the scales.

But there are no doubt going to be ways to slant these mind-reading scans, Greely says. Someone could perhaps fake the test by vividly remembering past pain, like the time they had a kidney stone or appendicitis.

Privacy, Bias, and Self-Incrimination

How can your brain be private when someone with a scanner could read its deepest secrets, including its state of health and your identity?

As sophisticated imaging of live brains in real time reveals more information that can be correlated to brain areas related to behavior and to health, it raises concerns about how this information could be used. Scans now can show signs of several diseases, such as Alzheimer's or schizophrenia, before symptoms appear and will no doubt be able to show more in the future. Will insurance companies demand scans before covering people and refuse those with preexisting brain conditions? Will law enforcement agencies ask for scanning of those accused of crimes or standing trial—or ask to scan brains of airline passengers for signs of terrorism? Will employers ask to scan brains for signs of bias as well as disease?

Will lawyers in turn invoke claims that constitutional rights are being violated by such tests: the Fourth Amendment against unlawful search and seizure, the Fifth Amendment against self-incrimination?

Protecting privacy in brain scans may be impossible. It's thought that everyone's brain (and thus brain images) is unique. Therefore, you could be identified by your brain scan just as you can be now by your DNA. That means there is no privacy guarantee for those who volunteer to be part of a brain scan study, even though they are told their identities won't be revealed.

Another ethical issue arises for the willing participants in brain scan studies. If a participant is found to have a serious neurological defect or disease not related at all to the study, are the researchers obliged to divulge this? In fact, are they obligated then to provide treatment?

Psychotreatment: Should We Force Psychopharmacological Therapies?

We already do it. Seven states require a brain intervention, chemical castration, as a condition of parole for those convicted of certain sex crimes, even though the drugs have side effects. Addicts and the mentally ill are forced to take drugs in some cases in exchange for freedom from incarceration. A vaccine against cocaine addiction is under development: Will addicts be forced to have this? Is it ethical (or legal) to force people to take such a vaccine—and thus deny them pleasure? Will we have to alter our brains chemically to keep competitive at our jobs, and will some employers require this as a condition of employment?

If you could successfully change somebody's brain, should you be able to? Even if you are changing it for the better or relieving it of disease? If you could turn antisocial beings into upright citizens, could you require it? How much further do we want to go?

Mental Doping on the Rise: They Jail Athletes, Don't They?

The illegal use of attention deficit hyperactivity disorder (ADHD) drugs to boost performance in healthy people has raised eyebrows and ethical issues. If steroids and other performance-enhancing drugs are illegal for athletes (human and equine), shouldn't neuroenhancing drugs also be banned when competition is involved? Because Ritalin and other ADHD drugs give students a mental edge (in focus and endurance at least), is it fair for students to use them in, say, taking the law school entrance exams?

There is a counterargument: Is this really different from the advantages given unevenly in terms of genetic blessings, supportive home environments, better nutrients, or parents willing to schlep fledgling athletic stars or music prodigies to their practice sessions and lessons?

Life is not fair. The question is, How much more unfair will mind-boosting drugs make it? In fact, some argue, it will level the playing field more, because those less mentally endowed (or who have less access to natural dopamine) get the biggest boost.

The pragmatic answer, of course is, What are you going to do about it? It would be at least as difficult to police mind drugs as athletic-boosting steroids—and we've all seen how effective that is.

Issues Yet to Come: A Future of Busy Lawyers

There's plenty more on the horizon.

The technology and treatments in the works and in planning are going to be very expensive, at least at first. Who will benefit from them: The rich and well connected? And who will determine who should get them? The so-called God committees that determine who get life-saving organ transplants are an example of how wrenching the allocation of limited, and expensive, treatment can be.

There's no doubt that the government, including the military, will get first crack, and that poses other concerns. The government is less constrained by legal and ethical rules than the rest of us and does not have to make some experiments public. For example, Greely notes, your employer (today at least) can't tell you that you must use amphetamines to improve your job performance, but the air force can—and does.

Ownership of your digital self is bound to become an issue, as is protecting the privacy and security of sensitive information stored digitally, including that in your brain chip. Will others be able to access your brain chip remotely? Can you be subpoenaed to have your memory chip "read" into testimony in court and criminal cases?

And think about how this digital you could continue to exist when your physical body is gone. It's possible your digital self could interact with your descendants. Interactive computer programs (of varying sophistication) still have a long way to go before they are "human," but the potential is there. Cloning humans, forbidden now, could grow a physical you to house that digital "brain." Actually some scientists have experimented with whole head transplants in animals, in which a host animal's body supported the extra, grafted head. Some years ago, a writer in *Scientific American* speculated this could become a reality for humans in the future. Creepy, but true.

Another question: Who is going to have access (and the password) to your digital brain after your physical self is gone? In fact, what is "self"? What about just wiping it all clean—or could that result in controversy similar to that about destroying frozen embryos?

And this doesn't even deal with the practicalities, such as keeping up with advancing technology to retrieve stored memories. Remember how CDs replaced eight-track tapes? No? How about when DVDs replaced videotapes?

New legal and ethical issues will arise with each new change in neuroscience and neurotechnology, just as they have in biology and medicine of the past—even the distant past.

But the issues generated by the advances in neuroscience and neurotechnology are special. They both overlap and outflank the ones raised by genetic engineering and other biomedical fields because they are different in one telling and overriding respect: They are tinkering with the very essence of what it means to be human.

Changing the brain with drugs, magnetic fields, surgery, or any other of the admittedly wonderful therapies could modulate the way we think—and feel—and may bend the very definition of who we are.

Even as we forge ahead in this brave new world of neuroscience, the potential for abuse prompts caution. As more than one commentator has noted, we know that the basis of what we each are is not all in our genes, but it is much more difficult to argue persuasively that it is not all in our heads.

CHAPTER TEN

The Past Is Prologue
To the Future

By now you know this is a book about wonder, possibilities, and promise.

The cutting-edge research described in the previous chapters is stretching our boundaries of knowledge and has already challenged and even overthrown many established dogmas of neuroscience. Indeed, science and technology are changing so rapidly that by the end of this century, there may be brain fixes that we or even science-fiction writers haven't begun to think of yet for ailing and healthy brains.

Most promising is the collaboration among the sciences. Who would have thought, even fifty years ago, that a physicist, materials scientist, engineer, and computer scientist would be working together with neurologists, biologists, psychologists, and biochemists on brain research? The work on artificial retinas that is giving vision to the blind is an outstanding example of scientific, institutional, and international cooperation.

But as fast as brain research is moving, it's important to remember that science is made up of incremental gains. Many of the predictions made here could take decades to become reality. We are still a long way from understanding most of the intricate workings of our most complex organ: Much of our brain science is still experimental or even theoretical. When some things go wrong, we aren't too sure why yet, let alone how to translate much of this exciting research into useful practice and therapies. In spite of the avalanche of new information and quite amazing new technologies, we still know very little about mental illness and autism, for example, and consciousness remains the largest mystery of all.

We're gaining on it. There's no doubt about that, and even the most conservative scientists have few doubts about where we are going. To paraphrase some science-fiction classics, we've embarked on a journey into the final frontier—our brain—to boldly go where no one has ever gone before. It's truly a fantastic voyage.

Introduction

Brain Science Is Big Business: Statistics about neurotechnology and business from Zack Lynch, "Neurotechnology Industry 2009 Report," http://brainwaves.corante.com/archives/2009/05/27/neurotechnology_industry_2009_report_released.php.

Chapter One: Your Changeable Brain

How Your Brain Changes: Adapted from multiple sources, including: Fred H. Gage, "Brain, Repair Yourself," *Scientific American*, Sept. 2003. Tracy J. Shors, "Saving New Brain Cells," *Scientific American*, Mar. 2009. R. Douglas Fields, "New Brain Cells Go to Work," *Scientific American Mind*, Aug.–Sept. 2007. Gary Stix, "Ultimate Self-Improvement," *Scientific American Special Edition: Better Brains*, Sept. 2003.

Your Brain Is a Computer: Adapted from Michael Shermer, "Why You Should Be Skeptical of Brain Scans," *Scientific American Mind*, Sept.–Oct. 2008.

Changes in Your Brain: Eleanor A. Maguire and others, "Navigation-Related Structural Change in the Hippocampi of Taxi Drivers," *Proceedings of the National Academy of Sciences of the United States of America*, Apr. 2000, http://www.pnas.org/content/97/8/4398.full.

Centenarians Rule: Adapted from the National Institute on Aging, "Unprecedented Global Aging Examined in New Census Bureau Report Commissioned by the National Institute on Aging," July 20, 2009, http://www.nia.nih.gov/NewsAndEvents/PressReleases/20090720global.htm.

Changes in Your Genes: Adapted from Edmund S. Higgins, "The New Genetics of Mental Illness," *Scientific American Mind*, June–July 2008. "Epigenomics," National Human Genome Research Institute at the National Institutes of Health, http://www.genome.gov/27532724. Jörn Walter, "Epigenetics," http://epigenome.eu/en/1,1,0.

Keeping Your New Brain Cells: Adapted from Shors, "Saving New Brain Cells."

Brain Training Programs: Adapted from Kaspar Mossman, "Brain Trainers," *Scientific American Mind*, Apr.–May 2009. Robert Goodier, "Brain Training's Unproven Hype," *Scientific American Mind*, July–Aug. 2009.

Peter J. Snyder, Kathryn V. Papp, Stephen J. Walsh, "Immediate and Delayed Effects of Cognitive Interventions in Healthy Elderly: A Review of Current Literature and Future Directions," *Alzheimer's & Dementia*, Jan. 2009, http://www.alzheimersanddementia.com/article/S1552-5260(08)02922-1/abstract.

Could Weight Gain Make You a Fathead? I. Soreca and others, "Gain in Adiposity Across 15 Years Is Associated with Reduced Gray Matter Volume in Healthy Women," *Psychosomatic Medicine: Journal of Biobehavioral Medicine*, May 29, 2009. N. L. Heard-Costa and others, "Nrxn3 Is a Novel Locus for Waist Circumference: A Genome-Wide Association Study from the Charge Consortium," *PLoS Genetics*, June 26, 2009, http://www.plosgenetics.org/.

Background: National Human Genome Research Institute, National Institutes of Health, http://www.genome.gov. National Institutes of Health, Roadmap Epigenomics Program, http://nihroadmap.nih.gov/epigenomics/. Epigenome Network of Excellence, http://www.epigenome-noe.net. W. Wayt Gibbs, "The Unseen Genome," *Scientific American*, Dec. 2003. Norman Dodge, *The Brain That Changes Itself* (New York: Penguin Books, 2007).

Chapter Two: Boosting Your Brain Power

Boosting Your Brain Power: Adapted from multiple sources, including: Gary Stix, "Turbocharging the Brain," *Scientific American*, Oct. 2009.

Ulrich Kraft, "Train Your Brain," *Scientific American Mind*, Feb. 2006.

Amir Levine, "Unmasking Memory Genes," *Scientific American Mind*, June–July 2008.

The Brave New Pharmacy: R. M. Scheffler and others, "Positive Association Between Attention Deficit/Hyperactivity Disorder Medication Use and Academic Achievement During Elementary School," *Pediatrics*, 2009, *123*(5), 1273–1279.

Juicing the Brain: Adapted from Christopher Intagliata, "Ritalin Dose Changes Effect," from 60-Second Science, *Scientific American Online*, July 9, 2008, http://www.scientificamerican.com/podcast/episode.cfm?id=081535BC-EB62-D649-01B40A271E2C0EDE.

The Caveats: Adapted from Edmund S. Higgins, "Do ADHD Drugs Take a Toll on the Brain?" *Scientific American Mind*, July–Aug. 2009. Benedetto Vitiello and Kenneth Towbin, "Stimulant Treatment of ADHD and Risk of Sudden Death in Children," *American Journal of Psychiatry*, 2009, *166*, 955–957.

Six Drug-Free Ways to Boost Your Brain: Adapted from Emily Anthes, "Six Ways to Boost Brain Power," *Scientific American Mind*, Feb.–Mar. 2009.

Meditation sections: Adapted from several sources: Jamie Talen, "Science Probes Spirituality," *Scientific American Mind*, Feb.–Mar. 2006. J. A. Brefczynski-Lewis and others, "Neural Correlates of Attentional Expertise in Long-Term Meditation Practitioners," *Proceedings of the National Academy of Sciences*, July 3, 2007. Richard J. Davidson and others, "Alterations in Brain and Immune Function Produced by Mindfulness Meditation," *Psychosomatic Medicine*, 2003, 65, 564–570. Antoine Lutz and others, "Long-Term Meditators Self-Induce High-Amplitude Gamma Synchrony During Mental Practice," *Proceedings of the National Academy of Sciences*, Nov. 16, 2004. Interviews and correspondence with Richard Davidson and Ferris Buck Urbanowski, 2009. Melissa A. Rosenkranz and others, "Affective Style and In Vivo Immune Response: Neurobehavioral Mechanisms," *Proceedings of the National Academy of Sciences*, Sept. 16, 2003.

Background: Kraft, "Train Your Brain." Jonathon D. Moreno, "Juicing the Brain," *Scientific American Mind*, Dec. 2006–Jan. 2007. Margaret Talbot, "The Underground World of 'Neuroenhancing' Drugs," *New Yorker*, Apr. 27, 2009. Herbert Benson, *The Relaxation Response* (New York: HarperTorch, 1976). Richard J. Davidson and Antoine Lutz, "Buddha's Brain: Neuroplasticity and Meditation," *IEEE Signal Processing Magazine*, Sept. 2007.

Chapter Three: Manipulating Your Memory

How Memory Works: Adapted from several articles by R. Douglas Fields: "Making Memories Stick," *Scientific American*, Feb. 2009. "New Brain Cells Go to Work," *Scientific American Mind*, Aug.–Sept. 2007. "Erasing Memories," *Scientific American Mind*, Dec. 2005–Jan. 2006. Amir Levine, "Unmasking Memory Genes," *Scientific American Mind*, June–July 2008.

Alzheimer's Disease: Statistics and basic information. Alzheimer's Disease International World Alzheimer Report, 2009, http://www.alz.co.uk/worldreport; Alzheimer's Association, http://www.alz.org/media_media_resources.asp.

Alzheimer's Disease Neuroimaging Initiative, http://www.adni-info.org/. "Measuring Brain Atrophy in Patients with Mild Cognitive Impairment," University of California, San Diego, news release, June 16, 2009. Joel Shurkin, "Alternative Ideas About Alzheimer's," *Scientific American Mind*, July–Aug. 2009.

What We Know Now About Dementia: Alzheimer's study in caregivers from C. Lyketsos and others, "Caregiver-Recipient Closeness and Symptom Progression in Alzheimer Disease. The Cache County Dementia Progression Study." *Journals of Gerontology Series B: Psychological Sciences and Social Sciences*, Sept. 2009. ACE study: Kaycee Sink, "Angiotensin-Converting Enzyme Inhibitors and Cognitive Decline in Older Adults with Hypertension: Results from the Cardiovascular Health Study," *Archives of Internal Medicine*, July 23, 2009. Alzheimer's and curcumin: Adapted from "Vitamin D, Curcumin May Help Clear Amyloid Plaques Found in Alzheimer's," news release, UCLA, July 15, 2009, http://newsroom.ucla.edu/portal/ucla/ucla-study-finds-vitamin-d-may-94903.aspx?link_page_rss=94903. Alzheimer's and cinnamon: Dylan W. Peterson and others, "Cinnamon Extract Inhibits Tau Aggregation Associated with Alzheimer's Disease in Vitro." *Journal of Alzheimer's Disease*, 2009, *17*(3). Alzheimer's and IVIg treatments: Howard Fillit and others, "IV Immunoglobulin Is Associated with a Reduced Risk of Alzheimer Disease and Related Disorders," *Neurology*, July 21, 2009. Alcohol study: Kaycee Sink and others, "Moderate Alcohol Intake Is Associated with Lower Dementia Incidence: Results from the Ginkgo Evaluation of Memory Study (GEMS)." Presented at Alzheimer's Association International Conference on Alzheimer's Disease, Vienna, July 13, 2009.

Marijuana to Ward Off Alzheimer's? Adapted from Andrew Klein, "Staving Off Dementia," *Scientific American Mind*, Apr.–May 2007.

Erasing Bad Memories: Michael S. Gazzaniga, "Smarter on Drugs," *Scientific American Mind*, Oct. 2005. M. H. Monfils, K. K. Cowansage, E. Klann, and J. S. LeDoux, "Extinction-Reconsolidation Boundaries: Key to Persistent Attenuation of Fear Memories," *Science*, May 15, 2009. Amir Levin, "Unmasking Memory Genes," *Scientific American Mind*, June–July 2008. CREB research: Christie Nicholson, "Wiping Out Bad Memories," *Scientific American Online*, http://www.scientificamerican.com/podcast/episode.cfm?id=wiping-out-bad-memories-09-03-08.

The Toll of Mental Illness: Peter Sergo, "Mental Illness in America," *Scientific American Mind*, Feb.–Mar. 2008. Interview with Joseph LeDoux: To learn more about his work, see http://www.cns.nyu.edu/ledoux/Ledouxlab.html.

What's Next? Excerpts from Amir Levine, "Unmasking Memory Genes," *Scientific American Mind*, June–July 2008.

Background: Cures for Alzheimer's: Vernon Vinge, *Rainbows End* (New York: Tor, 2006). Statistics on military suicides: Erica Goode, "Suicide's Rising Toll: After Combat, Victims of an Inner War," *New York Times*, Aug. 1, 2009. Alzheimer's disease statistics and basic information as of July 2009: Alzheimer's Association, http://www.alz.org/media_media_resources.asp. Alzheimer's Disease Neuroimaging Initiative, http://www.adni-info.org/. Statistics on the annual cost of prescription drugs to treat Alzheimer's: *New York Times* news reports, 2009.

Chapter Four: Digital You

Cell Phone Statistics: Pew Internet & American Life Project, http://www.pewinternet.org/Reports/2009/12-Wireless-Internet-Use.aspx.

Are You Born Digital—or a Digital Immigrant? Marc Prensky, "Digital Natives, Digital Immigrants," *On the Horizon*, 2001, *9*(5).

The Brains of Digital Natives: Information from Digital Native project: Beckman Center for Internet and Society at Harvard University and the Research Center for Information Law at the University of St. Gallen in Switzerland, http://www.digitalnative.org/#home. John Palfrey and Urs Gasser, *Born Digital: Understanding the First*

Generation of Digital Natives (New York: Basic Books, 2008). Digital media and teen interactivity statistics: Pew Internet & American Life Project, http://www.pewinternet. org/.

The Bad, the Good, and the Unknown Effects of Technology: Gary Small and Gigi Vorgan, *iBrain: Surviving the Technological Alteration of the Modern Mind* (New York: HarperCollins, 2008). G. W. Small, T. D. Moody, P. Siddarth, and S. Y. Bookheimer, "Your Brain on Google: Patterns of Cerebral Activation During Internet Searching," *American Journal of Geriatric Psychiatry*, 2009, *17*(2). T. D. Moody, H. Gaddipati, G. W. Small, and S. Y. Bookheimer, *Neural Activation Patterns in Older Adults Following Internet Training*, presented at the 2009 Society for Neuroscience Meeting, Oct. 2009. K. Slegers, M. van Boxtel, and J. Jolles, "Effects of Computer Training and Internet Usage on Cognitive Abilities in Older Adults: A Randomized Controlled Study," *Aging Clinical and Experimental Research*, Feb. 2009, *21*(1), 43–54.

How Cell Phones Affect Your iBrain: R. Douglas Fields, "Call Me Sleepless," *Scientific American Mind*, Aug.–Sept. 2008.

The Future Is Closer Than You Think: Vernor Vinge, *Rainbows End* (New York: Tor, 2006).

Uses of the Digital You: DARPA LifeLog project, http://www.darpa.mil/. "FACT FILE: A Compendium of DARPA Programs" and "LifeLog Projects," http://www.defensetech. org/archives/000427.html.

What About My Body? Adapted in part from Charmaine Liebertz, "Think Better: Learning to Focus," *Scientific American Mind*, Dec. 2005–Jan. 2006. Statement recommending no television for toddlers from the American Academy of Pediatrics: http:// www.aap.org/sections/media/toddlerstv.htm.

Beyond Digital: Adapted from Melinda Wenner, "The Serious Need for Play," *Scientific American Mind*, Feb.–Mar. 2009. Peter B. Gray, "Play as a Foundation for Hunter-Gatherer Social Existence," *American Journal of Play*, Spring 2009, *1*(4).

What's Next? Gordon Bell and Jim Gemmell, "A Digital Life," *Scientific American*, Mar. 2007.

Happiness Is Contagious: Adapted from Adam Hinterthuer, *Scientific American* 60-second podcast, Dec. 5, 2008, http://www.scientificamerican.com/podcast/episode. cfm?id=happiness-is-contagious-08-12-05.

Background: Institute for the Future, "2009 Ten-Year Forecast, Civil Society: Networked Citizens," http://www.iftf.org/node/3008. Gary Small and Gigi Vorgan, "Meet Your iBrain," *Scientific American Mind*, Oct.–Nov. 2008, and *iBrain: Surviving the Technological Alteration of the Modern Mind*. Ray Kurzweil, "The Coming Merger of Man and Machine," *Scientific American Special Edition: Your Future with Robots*, Feb. 2008. Nicholas Carr, "Is Google Making Us Stupid?" *Atlantic*, July–Aug. 2008, http:// www.theatlantic.com/doc/200807/google. Face-to-face learning: From A. N. Meltzoff, P. K. Kuhl, J. Movellan, and T. Sejnowski, "Foundations for a New Science of Learning," *Science*, July 17, 2009, http://www.sciencemag.org/cgi/content/full/sci;325/5938/284.

Chapter Five: Looking Inside Your Brain

Smile, Say Cheese? Michael Shermer, "Why You Should Be Skeptical of Brain Scans," *Scientific American Mind*, Oct.–Nov. 2008.

Picture This: "Imaging People with Psychopathy," *Kings College London News*, Aug. 4, 2009, http://www.kcl.ac.uk/news/news_details.php?news_id=1137&year=2009. Pedophile study cited by Melinda Wenner, "Finding Connections," *Scientific American Mind*, Apr.–May 2009. "Imaging Study Finds Evidence of Brain Abnormalities in Toddlers with Autism," *Study in Archives of General Psychiatry*, May 4, 2009. Scanning the Other Half of Your Brain: Adapted from Melinda Wenner, "Finding Connections," *Scientific American Mind*, Apr.–May 2009. Interview with R. Douglas Fields.

The Limits of Brain Scans: Shermer, "Why You Should Be Skeptical of Brain Scans." Edward Vul, C. Harris, P. Winkielman, and H. Pashler, "Puzzlingly High Correlations in fMRI Studies of Emotion, Personality, and Social Cognition," *Perspectives on Psychological Science*, 2009, 4(4), 285.

The Five Flaws of Brain Scans: Shermer, "Why You Should Be Skeptical of Brain Scans."

Do You See What I See? Excerpted from Nikhil Swaminathan, "Do You See What I See?" *Scientific American*, May 2008.

Virtually There: From George Kovacik, "New Technology Offers Virtual Visualization of the Human Body," Methodist Hospital, Houston, press release, July 1, 2009.

What's Next? Star Trek medical devices: From the StarTrek.com Library, http://www.startrek.com/startrek/view/library/science/article/69235.html.

Background: National Institute on Drug Abuse, Robert Mathias, "The Basics of Brain Imaging," http://www.drugabuse.gov/NIDA_notes/NNvol11N5/Basics.html. Margaret Talbot, "Duped: Can Brain Scans Uncover Lies?" *New Yorker*, July 2, 2007, http://www.newyorker.com/reporting/2007/07/02/070702fa_fact_Talbot. Bernhard Blumich, "The Incredible Shrinking Scanner," *Scientific American*, Nov. 2008. R. Douglas Fields, *The Other Brain* (New York: Simon & Schuster, 2009); for more information, visit http://theotherbrainbook.com/.

Chapter Six: Rewiring the Brain Electric

Electroshock's Shocking History: Excerpted from Morton L. Kringelbach and Tipu Z. Aziz, "Sparking Recovery with Brain 'Pacemakers,'" *Scientific American Mind*, Dec. 2008–Jan. 2009. John Horgan, "The Forgotten Era of Brain Chips," *Scientific American*, Oct. 2005.

The Current Brain Research: Adapted from Kringelbach and Aziz, "Sparking Recovery with Brain 'Pacemakers.'" tDCS therapy: R. Lindenberg, L. L. Zhu, V. Renga, D. Nair, and G. Schlaug, "Behavioral and Neural Effects of Bihemispheric Brain Stimulation on Stroke Recovery," abstract presented at the Fifteenth Annual Meeting of the Organization for Brain Mapping, Jan. 2009, http://www. meetingassistant3.com/OHBM2009/planner/abstract_popup.php?abstractno=1754. Adapted from Erica Westly, "A Magnetic Boost: Activating Certain Neurons May Alleviate Depression," *Scientific American Mind*, Apr.–May 2008. Hubertus Breuer, "A Great Attraction," *Scientific American Mind*, July 2005.

Discovering Depression's Sweet Spot: David Dobbs, "Turning Off Depression," *Scientific American Mind*, Aug.–Sept. 2006. David Dobbs, "Insights into the Brain's Circuitry," *Scientific American Mind*, Apr.–May 2009.

Melinda Wenner, "Finding Connections," *Scientific American Mind*, Apr.–May 2009.

Turn It Up, Dear, and Turn Me On: Adapted from Gary Stix, "Turn It Up, Dear," *Scientific American,* May 2009. Stuart Meloy Web site: http://www.aipmnc.com/NASF. aspx.

What's Next? Gero Miesenbock, "Lighting Up the Brain," *Scientific American*, Oct. 2008. Kringelbach and Aziz, "Sparking Recovery with Brain 'Pacemakers.'" Dobbs, "Insights into the Brain's Circuitry."

Background: Basic brain information and links: http://brainmapping.org.

Chapter Seven: Your Bionic Brain

Gary Stix, "Jacking into the Brain," *Scientific American*, Nov. 2008.

Frank W. Ohl and Henning Scheich, "Chips in Your Head," *Scientific American Mind*, Apr.–May 2007.

Anna Griffith, "Chipping In," *Scientific American*, Feb. 2007.

John Horgan, "The Forgotten Era of Brain Chips," *Scientific American*, Oct. 2005.

T. Kuiken and others, "Targeted Muscle Reinnervation for Real-Time Myoelectric Control of Multifunction Artificial Arms," *JAMA*, 2009, *301*, 619–628.

Artificial Retinas: Based on U.S. Department of Energy, Artificial Retina Project, http://artificialretina.energy.gov/; and on Second Sight Medical Products, http://www.2-sight.com/. Kwabena Boahen, "Neuromorphic Microchips," *Scientific American*, May 2005.

An Artificial Hippocampus? Gary Stix, "Jacking into the Brain," *Scientific American*, Nov. 2008.

Putting Thoughts into Action: Adapted from Alan S. Brown, "Putting Thoughts into Action," *Scientific American Mind*, Oct.–Nov. 2008. Interview with Philip R. Kennedy, founder of Neural Signals, a research and development company working on assistive technology, http://www.neuralsignals.com/.

Not Tonight, Dear: From Charles Q. Choi, "Not Tonight, Dear, I Have to Reboot," *Scientific American*, Mar. 2008.

What's Next? Ray Kurzweil, "The Coming Merger of Man and Machine," *Scientific American Presents Your New Mind*, June 2009.

Background: Miguel A. L. Nicolelis and John K. Chapin, "Controlling Robots with the Mind," *Scientific American Special Edition: Your Future with Robots*, Feb. 2008. Information on the Defense Advanced Research Projects Agency funding for neuroengineering, http://www.sciencedaily.com/releases/2002/08/020820071329. htm. MyLifeBits, Microsoft research project with Gordon Bell, http://research. microsoft.com/en-us/projects/mylifebits/#VannevarBush.

Chapter Eight: The Possible Dreams

Nanotechnology: James R. Heath, Mark E, Davis, and Leroy Hood, "Nanomedicine Targets Cancer," *Scientific American*, Feb. 2009.

Blood Will Tell: James R. Heath, Mark E. Davis, and Leroy Hood, "Nanomedicine Targets Cancer," *Scientific American*, Feb. 2009. David Dobbs, "Insights into the Brain's Circuitry," *Scientific American Mind*, Apr.–May, 2009.

The Future of Stem Cells: California Institute for Regenerative Medicine (stem cell research), http://www.cirm.ca.gov/?q=StemCellBasics; and 2009 interviews and correspondence with Donald Gibbons, CIRM chief communications officer. Batten Disease: "Researchers to Study Effectiveness of Stem Cell Transplant in Human Brain," *Science Daily*, Mar. 11, 2006.

Fixing Strokes with Stem Cells: Nikhil Swaminathan, "Stem Cells Against Stroke," *Scientific American*, Nov. 2008.

Retinal Stem Cells from Adults Show Promise: Adapted from Katherine Harmon, "Stem Cells Bring New Insights to Future Treatment of Vision—and Neural—Disorders," *Scientific American Online*, Sept. 24, 2009, http://www.scientificamerican. com/blog/post.cfm?id=stem-cells-bring-new-insights-to-fu-2009-09-24.

The Promise of Gene Therapy: Melina Wenner, "Regaining Lost Luster," *Scientific American*, Jan. 2008.

A Genetics Refresher: Heath, Davis, and Hood, "Nanomedicine Targets Cancer."

Epigenomics: National Human Genome Research Institute, http://www.genome. gov/27532724. The NIH Roadmap Epigenomics Program, http://nihroadmap.nih.gov/ epigenomics/.

Nanomedicine: From Heath, Davis, and Hood, "Nanomedicine Targets Cancer."

Background: California Institute for Regenerative Medicine (stem cell research), http://www.cirm.ca.gov/?q=StemCellBasics. National Human Genome Research

Institute, National Institutes of Health in Bethesda, Maryland, http://www.
genome.gov/. American Society of Gene and Cell Therapy, http://www.asgt.org/
educational_resources/. The National Nanotechnology Institute, http://www.nano.
gov/. Nanoparticle and stem cell research: Victor Stern, "Nanoparticles Spur Stem
Cells?" *TheScientist.com*, Oct. 7, 2009, http://www.the-scientist.com/blog/browse/
blogger/69/.

Chapter Nine: Neuroethics

Michael S. Gazzaniga, "The Law and Neuroscience," *Neuron*, Nov. 6, 2008, pp. 412–
415.

The Editors, "A Vote for Neuroethics: Better Brains," *Scientific American Special Issue*,
Sept. 2003. MacArthur Foundation Law and Neuroscience Project, with references to
many recent articles: http://www.lawandneuroscienceproject.org/.

Stem Cells: The Editors, "Opinion: Reality Check for Stem Cells," *Scientific American*,
June 2009.

Interview with Hank T. Greely, Deane F. and Kate Edelman Johnson Professor of Law
at Stanford University, Aug. 2009.

Liar, Liar: Interviews with Paul Ekman, Oct. 2009. Henry T. Greely and Judy Illes,
"Neuroscience-Based Lie Detection: The Urgent Need for Regulation," *American
Journal of Law and Medicine*, 2007, *33*, 377–431; quote from p. 402.

Responsibility: Michael Shermer, "Why You Should Be Skeptical of Brain Scans,"
Scientific American Mind, Oct.–Nov. 2008; Gary Stix, "Lighting Up the Lies," *Scientific
American*, Aug. 2008.

The Business of Brain Scans: Brain fingerprinting, http://web.archive.org/
web/20060722001256/http://www.ocf.berkeley.edu/~issues/spring03/brainfinger.
html. EEG used in trials: Nitasha Natu, "This Brain Test Maps the Truth," *Times of
India*, July 2008, http://timesofindia.indiatimes.com/Cities/This_brain_test_maps_
the_truth/articleshow/3257032.cms. No Lie MRI, http://www.noliemri.com/. Cephos
Corp., http://www.cephoscorp.com/.

Background: Mark A. Rothstein, "Keeping Your Genes Private," *Scientific American*,
Sept. 2008. Neuroscience, Law and Government Symposium, University of Akron,
Akron Law Review, 2008–2009, *42*(3). Hank T. Greely, "Law and the Revolution in
Neuroscience: An Early Look at the Field," keynote address at the Akron School of
Law's Neuroscience, Law and Government Symposium, *Akron Law Review*, 2008–
2009, *42*(3). MacArthur Foundation Law and Neuroscience Project Blog, http://
lawneuro.typepad.com/the-law-and-neuroscience-blog/. Project homepage, with
references to many recent articles: http://www.lawandneuroscienceproject.org/.
Stanford Center for Law and the Biosciences Blog, http://lawandbiosciences.
wordpress.com/about/.

ILLUSTRATION CREDITS

Some of Your Brain's Most Important Parts: Courtesy Alzheimer's Disease Education and Referral Center, a service of the National Institute on Aging.

Neurons: Your Brain Cells at Work: Courtesy Alzheimer's Disease Education and Referral Center, a service of the National Institute on Aging.

How the Brain Makes New Neurons: From Fred H. Gage, "Brain, Repair Yourself," *Scientific American*, Sept. 2003. Artist: Alice Chen.

How Learning Helps to Save New Neurons: From Tracy J. Shors, "Saving New Brain Cells," *Scientific American*, Mar. 2009. Artist: Jen Christiansen.

Epigenetics: Volume Control for Your Genes: From W. Wayt Gibbs, "The Unseen Genome: Beyond DNA," *Scientific American*, Dec. 2003. Artist: Terese Winslow.

How Brain Enhancers Work: From Gary Stix, "Turbocharging the Brain," *Scientific American*, Oct. 2009. Artist: Andrew Swift.

The Memory Code: A Seat of Memory: From Joe Z. Tsien, "The Memory Code," *Scientific American*, July 2007. Artist: Alice Chen.

What Is White Matter? From R. Douglas Fields, "White Matter Matters," *Scientific American*, Mar. 2008. Artist: Jen Christiansen.

An Artificial Hippocampus: From Gary Stix, "Jacking into the Brain," *Scientific American*, Nov. 2008. Artist: George Retseck.

Sparking Recovery with Brain Pacemakers: From Morten L. Kringelbach and Tipu Z. Aziz, "Sparking Recovery with Brain 'Pacemakers,'" *Scientific American Mind*, Dec. 2008/Jan. 2009. Artist: Melissa Thomas.

Targeted Magnetic Brain Stimulation: From Hubertus Breuer, "A Great Attraction," *Scientific American Mind*, June 2005. Artist: Bryan Christie Design.

The Future of Optogenetic Brain Stimulation: From Gero Misenböck, "Lighting Up the Brain," *Scientific American*, Oct. 2008. Artist: Alfred T. Kamajian.

An Artificial Retina: Copyright © 2009 The New York Times Company.

Spinal Cord Responsibilities: From Ulrich Kraft, "Mending the Spinal Cord," *Scientific American Mind*, Oct. 2005. Artist: Melissa Thomas.

The Origins and Fates of Embryonic Stem Cells: From Clive Cookson, "Special Report: The Future of Stem Cells," *Scientific American* and *Financial Times*, 2005. Artists: Andrew Swift, Robert P. Lanza.

GLOSSARY

acetylcholine—a neurotransmitter chemical that appears to regulate memory and controls skeletal and smooth muscle action in the peripheral nervous system.

adenosine—a neurochemical that is part of adenosine triphosphate (ATP), the energy mechanism that fuels cell metabolism. It's released with each ATP action, building up in the body and making you sleepy. When your body is sleeping, adenosine levels dwindle, helping you awaken.

ADHD (attention deficit hyperactivity disorder)—a condition that makes it difficult to remain focused mentally and physically. Often connected with learning disabilities or other mental problems.

adrenaline—a hormone and neurotransmitter that boots up the body to participate in the fight-or-flight response of the sympathetic nervous system. Also known as *epinephrine*.

ALS (amyotrophic lateral sclerosis, sometimes called Lou Gehrig's disease)—an always fatal condition in which nerves that control the body gradually die, leading to paralysis and death.

Alzheimer's disease—a progressive, neurodegenerative disease similar to dementia caused by cell death in several areas of the brain.

amphetamine—a psychostimulant drug that prompts wakefulness and focus and is the basis of many drugs for treating attention deficit hyperactivity disorder. Also known as *speed*.

amygdala—the survival-oriented part of the brain that regulates primitive emotions and the fight-or-flight syndrome. Sometimes called the *emotional brain*.

amyloid plaques—deposits found in the spaces between nerve cells in the brain that are made of beta-amyloid and other materials; believed to contribute to Alzheimer's disease.

SOURCE: This information was complied with permission from glossaries and informational articles of the several National Institutes of Health.

angiotensin-converting enzyme (ACE) inhibitors—medication prescribed for lowering blood pressure.

axon—the long extension from a neuron that transmits outgoing signals to other cells.

beta-amyloid protein—part of the amyloid precursor protein found in plaques, the insoluble deposits outside neurons.

bionic—using artificial parts to enhance or substitute for biological body parts or functions.

blood-brain barrier (BBB)—a process by which most materials, including bacteria, in the circulating bloodstream are blocked from entering the brain.

brain pacemaker—an electrode implanted into the brain that responds to electrical signals sent from a battery-operated control; used to control seizures or tremors from epilepsy or Parkinson's disease.

Broca's area—located in the left frontal lobe, this area controls facial neurons, speech, and understanding language.

Brodmann area 25—appears to connect several brain regions involved in mood, thought, and emotion and is hyperactive in depressed patients.

cannabinoids—chemicals produced naturally by the body that help control mental and physical processes, and that occur in marijuana; they produce intoxication when from marijuana.

cerebellum—two peach-size mounds of folded tissue located at the top of the brain stem that control skilled, coordinated movement (such as returning a tennis serve) and are involved in some learning pathways.

cerebral cortex—the outer 3 millimeters of gray matter that consist of closely packed neurons that control most body functions, including the mysterious state of consciousness, the senses, the body's motor skills, reasoning, and language.

cerebrum—the "thinking brain"; accounts for about two-thirds of the brain's mass and is positioned over and around most other brain structures. It's divided into two hemispheres (*see* corpus callosum), has four lobes, and is crowned by the cerebral cortex.

chemobrain—a common term for the fuzzy or otherwise impaired thinking that may accompany chemotherapy treatments.

cingulate nucleus—an area in the brain dealing with shifting attention among thoughts and conflict.

cloning—the process of making an exact DNA duplicate of another organism, organ, or cell.

computed tomography (CT) scan—a diagnostic imaging procedure that uses special X-ray equipment and computers to create cross-sectional pictures of the body.

corpus callosum—a fibrous bundle of axons that connects the two hemispheres of the brain.

deep brain stimulation (DBS)—stimulating or interrupting brain activity with electricity applied to electrodes implanted in the brain; may be connected to a computer or a battery.

dementia—a broad term referring to a decline in cognitive function to the extent that it interferes with daily life and activities.

dentate gyrus—a part of the hippocampus thought to contribute to the formation of memories; one of the few regions of the adult brain where neurogenesis is known to take place.

DNA (deoxyribonucleic acid)—a nucleic acid inherited from ancestors that makes up a person's genome (or genetics) and contains the instructions for making his or her unique body and brain. *See* RNA.

dopamine—a neurotransmitter vital for voluntary movement, attentiveness, motivation, and pleasure; a key player in the reward circuit and addiction.

DTI (diffusion tensor imaging)—measures the flow of water molecules along the white matter, or myelin, that makes up 50 percent of the brain and connects many regions. The technology is not yet easily interpreted.

dual-hemisphere transcranial direct current stimulation (tDCS)—a technique that uses electrical stimulation to modulate brain activity at the same time as the limb affected by the stroke is getting occupational therapy.

dystonia—a neurological movement disorder in which muscle contractions cause twisting and repetitive movements or abnormal postures.

electroencephalography (EEG)—a method of detecting and recording brain activity from electrodes placed on the scalp.

electroshock therapy (EST)—a process by which electrodes placed on the skull pass a current through the brain, causing a brief seizure and some changes in brain chemistry that ease symptoms of several kinds of mental illness. Sometimes called *electroconvulsive shock therapy*.

EMG (electromyography)—a method of detecting and recording tiny electrical potentials that are produced by muscles and the nervous system when muscles contract.

epigenetics—changes in gene expression or appearance, but not the underlying DNA sequence, caused by experiences or environment.

epigenome—the overall epigenetic state of a cell, similar to your genome but separate. *See* epigenetics.

FDA—U.S. Food and Drug Administration.

frontal lobe—the most recently evolved part of the brain and the last to develop in young adulthood; is responsible for so-called executive higher functions, including decision making, problem solving, thinking, planning, and verbal skills.

functional electrical stimulation (FES)—mild electrical shocks given to paralyzed muscles to make them move; sends messages up to the brain to help it rewire itself and relearn how to move the affected muscles.

functional magnetic resonance imaging (fMRI)—a type of brain scan that can be used to monitor the brain's activity and detect abnormalities in how it works.

gene—a segment of DNA found on a chromosome that acts as a blueprint for making virtually every biomedical reaction and structure in the body.

gene therapy—an evolving technique used to treat inherited diseases by replacing, manipulating, or supplementing nonfunctional genes with healthy genes.

genome—the sum of all the genes that code for a particular organism, such as the body and brain.

glial cells (also, glia, from glue in Greek)—specialized cells that make up the so-called white matter in the brain; provide support to neurons and electrical insulation between neurons and other functions not yet understood.

hippocampus—a structure located deep within the brain that plays a major role in learning and memory and is involved in converting short-term to long-term memory.

histones—small, basic proteins found in chromosomes that bind to DNA and help control the activities of genes.

hypothalamus—a structure in the brain under the thalamus that monitors activities such as body temperature and food intake, blood pressure, and other body functions.

limbic system—a brain region that links the brain stem with the higher-reasoning elements of the cerebral cortex; controls emotions, instinctive behavior, and the sense of smell.

magnetic resonance imaging (MRI)—a diagnostic and research technique that uses magnetic fields to generate a computer image of internal structures in the body; particularly good for imaging the brain and soft tissues.

myelin—"white matter": a whitish, fatty insulating layer surrounding an axon that helps it rapidly transmit electrical messages from the cell body to the synapse.

nano—a prefix meaning "very small, minute." A nanometer is one-billionth of a meter, too small to be seen with a conventional lab microscope.

nanobot—a miniscule robot; part of nanotechnology.

nanotechnology—the creation and use of materials and devices at the very small level of molecules and atoms.

neural—anything related to neurons, which are brain cells.

neurogenesis—the creation of new brain cells (neurons).

neuron—a brain or nerve cell.

neuroplasticity—the brain's ability to change in response to the environment, including thoughts and feelings, and to reassign some of its parts to take over new tasks.

neurotransmitter—a chemical messenger between neurons, released by the axon on one neuron to excite or inhibit activity in a neighboring neuron.

neurotrophic—having an affinity for or localizing selectively in nerve tissue.

neurotrophic electrode—a tiny device implanted onto a target area in the brain to detect neural activity.

nucleus accumbens—part of the brain's reward system, located in the limbic system, that processes information related to motivation and reward. Virtually all drugs of abuse act on the nucleus accumbens to reinforce drug taking.

obsessive-compulsive disorder (OCD)—an anxiety disorder characterized by obsessive thoughts and compulsive actions, such as cleaning, checking, counting, or hoarding.

occipital lobe—processes and routes visual data to other parts of the brain for identification and storage.

orbitofrontal cortex—part of the cerebral cortex; involved in making decisions and other cognitive processes.

plasticity—the ability of the brain to change through the formation or strengthening of connections between neurons in the brain.

positron emission tomography (PET)—an imaging technique using radioisotopes that allows researchers to observe and measure activity in different parts of the brain by monitoring blood flow and concentrations of substances such as oxygen and glucose, as well as other specific components of brain tissues.

prion—a rogue protein that co-ops normal proteins; responsible for a number of degenerative brain diseases, including Creutzfeldt-Jakob disease (mad cow disease).

psychosurgery—surgery on the brain or nervous system to change behavior, emotions, or character; may include deep brain stimulation.

retinal pigment epithelium (RPE)—a layer of tissue at the base of the retina that comes into being within thirty to fifty days of conception and is a possible source of stem cells.

RNA (ribonucleic acid)—similar to DNA; delivers DNA's genetic message to the cytoplasm of a cell, where proteins are made.

serotonin—a neurotransmitter that helps regulate body temperature, memory, emotion, sleep, appetite, and mood.

synapse—the tiny gap between neurons across which neurotransmitters and electrical charges pass.

tau protein—a key player in the development of Alzheimer's disease. Healthy tau supports neuron activity, but modified tau is believed to contribute to the brain tangles associated with Alzheimer's disease.

temporal lobe—brain area that controls the memory storage area, emotion, hearing, and—on the left side—language.

tetrahydrocannabinol (THC)—the psychoactive active ingredient in marijuana.

thalamus—located at the top of the brain stem. Acts as a two-way relay station, sorting, processing, and directing signals from the spinal cord and midbrain structures up to the cerebrum, and, conversely, from the cerebrum down the spinal cord to the nervous system.

Tourette's syndrome—a genetic nervous system disorder characterized by uncontrollable outbursts of often inappropriate words, movements, or noises.

transcranial magnetic stimulation (TMS)—applying mild electrical current to the outside of the brain to stimulate activity and treat some conditions such as depression.

ventral tegmental area (VTA)—located in the midbrain at the top of the brain stem; one of the most primitive parts of the brain. It synthesizes dopamine, which is sent to the nucleus accumbens.

Judith Horstman is an award-winning journalist who writes about health and medicine for doctors as well as the general public. Her work has appeared in hundreds of publications worldwide and on the Internet.

A long-time print journalist, she was the recipient of a Knight Science Journalism Fellowship at MIT, was a journalism professor at Oregon State University, and was awarded two Fulbright grants to establish a center to teach fact-based journalism in Budapest, Hungary.

She has edited a Web site for researchers and physicians on amyotrophic lateral sclerosis (also known as Lou Gehrig's disease), was a consultant and writer for a lupus Web site, and has written for the Stanford University Medical Center, the *Harvard Health Letter,* the Johns Hopkins University White Papers, and Time Inc. Health publications. She was also a contributing editor for *Arthritis Today,* the magazine of the Arthritis Foundation. She has been a Washington correspondent for the Gannett News Service and *USA Today,* where her work included articles on medicine and health policy.

This is her second brain book. Horstman is the author of *The Scientific American Day in the Life of Your Brain* (Jossey-Bass, 2009), as well as *The Arthritis Foundation's Guide to Alternative Therapies* and *Overcoming Arthritis* (with Paul Lam). Visit her Web site at www. judithhorstman.com.

About *Scientific American*

Scientific American is the world's leading source and authority for science and technology information. Since 1845, its magazines have chronicled the world's major science and technology innovations and discoveries. Published in nineteen foreign-language editions with a total circulation of more than 1 million worldwide, *Scientific American* reaches business executives, opinion leaders, policymakers, academics, and well-educated general consumers. *Scientific American* is also a leading online science, health, and technology destination (www.SciAm.com), providing the latest news and exclusive features to more than 1.7 million visitors monthly and distributing its content through podcasts and other digital services.

INDEX

A

Abnormal tau (brain tangles), 43

ACE (angiotensin-converting enzyme) inhibitors, 43

Acetyl groups, 53

Acetylcholine, 24, 44

Adderall, 23, 24

Addictions: dependence gene related to, 18; digital social, 65; gender differences in video game, 30

ADHD (attention deficit hyperactivity disorder): cortical development in young people with, 27; drug treatment of, 22–24, 27–28; implant research on, 90; psychopharmacy used for, 22–24; similarities of digital natives with, 59; underactive frontal cortex and, 25. *See also* Children

ADHD drugs: brain stimulation by, 30; effects and black market on, 22–23; memory enhancement of, 46, 48; neuroethics related to, 136–137; studies on safety of, 27–28

Adrenaline, 25, 46

Alcohol: dependence gene related to abuse of, 18; research on Alzheimer's disease and, 44

"Allegory of the Cave" (Plato), 84

Allen, W., 97

ALS (amyotrophic lateral aclerosis), 103, 105, 125

Alzheimer Disease Neuroimaging Initiative, 41

Alzheimer's & Dementia (journal), 18

Alzheimer's disease: abnormal tau hallmark of, 43; hippocampus damage from, 109; implants used to treat, 96, 103; marijuana to prevent, 44–45; memory affected by, 41–42; neurotransmitter acetylcholine to treat, 24; prevention and treatment of, 43–44; promise of stem cells or gene replacement for, 127; *Rainbows End* (Vinge) novel on, 41–42, 61–62; research on, 2, 19, 92, 102; then, now, and tomorrow research on, 6. *See also* Dementia

American Journal of Law and Medicine, 133

Amphetamine methylphenidate, 24

Amphetamines, 24

Amygdala: autistic children and larger size, 77; description and function of, 4; DTI scanning to find anomalies in the, 76–77; fear, consolidating memory, and, 46;

meditation effect on, 12–13; understanding limits of scanning the, 83

Animal studies: on artificial hippocampus, 109; on brain cells and effortful new learning, 16–17; on drug effects on the brain, 28; erasing memories, 49; eyeblink course, 15–16; on growth of brain cells, 15; HDAC inhibitors and learning, 53; lowering risk of Alzheimer's disease, 44; on mad cow disease, 119; PKMzeta, 50; on radio-equipped electrodes implants, 89; on repair of spinal cord injury, 121; restoring memories, 54; on Ritalin dosage, 25–26. *See also* Brain research

Antidepressants, 25, 43

Anxiety disorders, 50–52

Aricept, 24

Aristotle, 132

Aromatherapy, 65

Artificial hippocampus research, 108–110

Artificial intelligence: movies on, 112; predictions on future of, 62; research on thought-driven devices and, 110–112

Artificial Intelligence (film), 112

Artificial retinas, 107–108

Atlantic Monthly, 60

Autistic children, 77

avatar, 62, 67, 103

Avatar (film), 116, 128

Aziz, T. Z., 91

B

Basal ganglia, 4

Batten disease (neuronal ceroid ipofuscinosis), 121

The Beatles, 32

Bell, G., 67–68

Benson, H., 33

Berger, T. W., 109

Berkman Center for Internet and Society (Harvard University), 58

Beta-amyloid proteins, 42, 43

Biological clock, 4

Biological Psychiatry (journal), 25

Bionic brain: brain-machine interface, cyborgs, "robot love" and, 104, 112, 113; current research being done on, 104–106; giving sight to the blind, 107–108; possible research breakthroughs on, 102–104; research on downloading information to, 106–107; science fiction versus realities of, 104; technical hurdles of creating a, 114–116; thought-driven devices and, 110–112. *See also* Implants/electrodes

The Bionic Woman (TV series), 104

Bipolar disorder, 50

Blood: body system health and state of, 119; nanotechnology and the blood-brain barrier, 126

Body play, 66

Born Digital: Understanding the First Generation of Digital Natives (Palfrey and Gasser), 58

Brain: blood-brain barrier of, 126; comparing computer and the human, 112, 114; digital social addiction of, 65; emotional (or limbic system), 4; how it changes, 7–20; short version of how it works, 3–4; stimulation or boosting the, 22–36; synapses of the, 39, 51, 78, 114; then, now, and tomorrow knowledge about, 5–6; thinking, 4; two hemispheres of, 4, 98; white matter (myelin) of the, 77–79. *See also* Brain fun facts

Brain anomalies: legal applications of, 134–136; phrenology (pseudoscience) identifying, 72; in psychopaths, pedophile, and autistic toddlers, 76–77, 78; summary of tools used for identifying, 73–74. *See also* Brain scans (neuroimaging)

Brain cells: animal studies on growth of, 15; epigenetics and, 8, 13–14; keeping your new, 14–16; neurogenesis production of new, 7–8, 10–11; neuroplasticity repair of, 8, 11–13; research on learning or practicing tasks and, 16–17. *See also* DNA (deoxyribonucleic acid)

Brain changes: epigenetics and, 8, 13–14, 19, 52, 53–54; future of research on, 19–20; MRI scans to measuring cerebral cortex, 27; neurogenesis and, 7–8, 10–11, 15–16, 19–20; neuroplasticity and, 8, 11–13, 19; research then, now, and tomorrow on, 8; ways in which the, 7–10

Brain drug-free stimulation: diet for, 29–30; exercise for, 29, 35; learning for, 30; meditation for, 13, 31–35; music for, 30–31; video games for, 30

Brain electrical activity: current available treatments for charging, 93; current brain research on, 90–95; emotions linked to, 88; EST (electroshock therapy), 49, 89, 93; FES (functional electrical stimulation), 93; future applications for manipulation of, 97–100; history of research on, 88–90; implants or electrodes for, 89, 90–95, 96, 97; tDCS (transcranial direct current stimulation), 93–94; TMS (transcranial magnetic stimulation), 92–93. *See also* DBS (deep brain stimulation)

Brain Fingerprinting, 135

Brain fun facts: blood as your inner highway, 119; brain-machine interface future, 113; brain's operation similar to Internet, 9; business of brain scans, 135; centenarian brains, 12; contagious nature of happiness, 69; decoding patterns in visual areas of the brain, 83; digital social addiction, 65; genetics refresher, 124; memory trick, 47; nootropes for mental boost, 23; Plato's cave technique (3-D video technology), 84; today's treatments for charging your brain, 93; tools for looking inside the brain, 73–74; what is meditation, 32. *See also* Brain; Movie boxes

Brain hemispheres: description of, 4; stimulating creativity by equalizing, 98

Brain research: on Alzheimer's disease and dementia, 2, 6, 19, 43–45, 92, 102; on bionic brain applications, 102–107, 114–116; on brain activity and Internet use, 59–61; on brain cells and effortful learning, 16–17; on brain electrical activity, 90–95, 97–100; on drug effects on the brain, 28; gene therapy related to, 118–125; on growth of brain cells, 15; on meditation effects on the brain, 33–35; nanomedicine related to, 125–127; on obesity and the brain, 18; on prompting neurogenesis, 19–20; rat eyeblink course, 15–16; on Ritalin dosage, 25–26;

stem cell research related to, 118–123; tremendous surge and promise of, 1–2, 141–142. *See also* Animal studies; Brain science; Neuroethics

Brain research (then, now, tomorrow): bionic brain, 102; boosting your brain power, 22; brain surgery, 6, 118; digital explosion and your iBrain, 56; electricity in the brain, 88; how the brain changes, 8; looking inside the brain, 72; manipulating your memory, 38; neuroethics, 130; overview of what we know about the brain, 5–6

Brain scans flaws: 1: studies are skewed by selection and environment, 80–81; 2: scans don't measure direct brain activity, 81; 3: the pretty colors are fake, 81–82; 4: that's not one brain: that's a statistic, 82; 5: there are many reasons that area activates, 82–83

Brain scans (neuroimaging): brain surgery and diagnostic role of, 72–73; used to diagnosis and treat brain anomalies, 76–77; DTI (diffusion tensor imaging), 74, 76–77, 78–79; five flaws of, 80–83; fMRI, 60, 74–76, 79–80, 81, 83, 133–134, 135; history of, 72; legal applications of, 134–136; lie detection using, 133–136; limits of, 79–80; MRI, 27, 42, 74–76, 79–80, 84, 133–136; Plato's cave technique (3-D video technology) for, 84; possible future uses and ethics of, 85–86; privacy, bias, and self-incrimination issues of, 136–137; summary of tools used for, 73–74; of white matter (myelin),

77–79. *See also* Brain anomalies; Technology

Brain science: as big business, 2–3; current and tomorrow advances in, 1–2; overview of past, present, future, 5–6; phrenology (pseudoscience), 72. *See also* Brain research

Brain stem (primitive brain or hindbrain), 3–4

Brain stimulant drugs. *See* Drugs

Brain stimulation: EST (electroshock therapy) for, 49, 89, 93; FES (functional electrical stimulation) for, 93; future applications of electrical, 97–100; nootrope products for, 23; possible future approaches of, 35–36; recreational drugs to increase, 23; six drug-free ways for, 29–35; "smart drugs" for juicing, 24–28; stimulant drugs used for, 22–24; tDCS (transcranial direct current stimulation) for, 93–94; then, now, and tomorrow research on, 22; TMS (transcranial magnetic stimulation) for, 92–93. *See also* DBS (deep brain stimulation); Implants/electrodes

Brain surgery: frontal lobotomy, 89, 90, 131; future predictions on, 2; neuroimaging role in, 72–73; past, current, and tomorrow of, 6, 118–121. *See also* DBS (deep brain stimulation); Implants/electrodes

Brain training programs, 17–19

Brain-machine interface. *See* Bionic brain

Brainstorm (film), 63

BrdU (bromodeoxyurdine), 15, 16

British Medical Journal, 69

Broca's area, 9

Brown University, 18, 111
"Bubble Boy" disease, 119
Bush, G. W., 132
Bush, V., 67
Butler, E. B., 84

C
Caffeine, 46
Caidin, M., 104
California Institute for Regenerative Medicine (CIRM), 121
Cannabinoids, 45
Carr, N., 60
Carrey, J., 49
Case Western Reserve University, 111
Castner, S. A., 28
CAT (computed axial tomography), 74
Cell phones, 61
Centenarian brains, 12
Cephos, 135
Cerebral cortex, 27
Charly (film), 26
Chemotherapy: chemobrain syndrome of, 10–11; nanoparticle delivery of, 126–127
Children: identifying anomalies related to autistic, 77; play crucial for development of, 66–67; research on digital technology and, 64; stem cell research on Batten disease in, 121. *See also* ADHD (attention deficit hyperactivity disorder)
Claudius (Roman Emperor), 87
Clinton, H., 82
Cloning, 128, 139
Coca-Cola, 23
Coca plant, 23
Cocaine: brain stimulation by, 30; dopamine effect by, 25; methylphenidate structure similarity to, 28

Cochlear implant, 106–107
Cognitive performance: animal studies on drugs and impaired, 28; childhood play for development of, 66–67; study on Internet impact on, 60–61
College students: ADHD "smart pills" taken by, 26–27; black market ADHD drugs taken by, 22–23
Communication: addiction to digital social, 65; cybercommunication form of, 60; DARPA investment in computer-mediated telepathy, 86; digital natives and shorthand, 58
Computer-brain comparison, 112, 114
Computer-mediated telepathy research, 86
Concerta, 24
Consciousness research, 6
Consolidation of memory, 46
Corpus callosum, 4
Council on Bioethics, 132
CREB (cyclic adenosine monophosphate response element-binding protein), 50
Crichton, M., 91
CT (computed tomography), 74
Curcumin (turmeric), 43
Cybermemory, 63
Cybernarcissism, 68
Cyborg (Caidin), 104
Cyborgs/robot love science fiction, 104, 112, 113

D
Dalai Lama, 33–34
DARPA. *See* U.S. Defense Advanced Research Projects Agency (DARPA)
Darwin, C., 78
Davidson, R., 34, 35–36

DBS (deep brain stimulation): boosting brain performance using, 35; as brain pacemaker, 91; depression treatment using, 95–96; description of, 93; diseases and mental disorders treated with, 92, 94; psychiatric disorder research on, 90; research on improving, 98–99. *See also* Brain electrical activity; Brain stimulation; Brain surgery

Deisseroth, K., 99

Delgados, J., 89

Dementia: national statistics on, 41; predictions on research related to, 2; research on preventing and treating, 43–44. *See also* Alzheimer's disease

Dendrite, 39

Dentate gyrus, 10

Depression: DBS treatment for, 95–96; research on stimulating neurons to allay, 111; TMS treatment for, 92–93. *See also* Mental illness

Dextroamphetamine, 24

Dick, P. K., 109

Diet: boosting your brain through, 29–30; memory enhancement through, 19

Digital immigrants, 56

Digital natives: ADHA similarities with, 59; brains and characteristics of, 57–59; description of, 56–57; digital social addiction of, 65; technology effects on, 59–61

Digital Natives (organization), 58

Digital social addiction, 65

Digital technology: bad, good, and unknown effects of, 59–61; balancing sensory self and iBrain of, 64–65; continuing interest and research on, 63; digital social addiction to, 65; future vision of, 61–62; interactive learning through, 58–59; *Rainbows End* (Vinge) on world of, 41–42, 61; speculations on future of, 67–69

Digital X-ray, 73

DNA (deoxyribonucleic acid): cloning and, 128, 139; epigenetics and, 13–14, 52, 53–54; genetics refresher on, 124. *See also* Brain cells; Genes

Donepezil, 24

Donoghue, J., 111, 115

Dopamine: ADHD drugs enhancing, 25; cocaine and methamphetamine blocking, 28

Drugs: ADHD treatment by, 22–24, 27–28, 46, 48, 137–138; brain stimulants or neuroenhancing, 22–24; cocaine, 25, 28, 30; marijuana, 44–45; nootrope products, 23; NSAIDs (nonsteroidal anti-inflammatory drugs), 43; recreational, 23; "smart drugs" for juicing the brain, 24–28

DTI (diffusion tensor imaging): of brain anomalies, 76–77; description of, 74; understanding mental illness through, 99; of white matter (myelin), 78–79

DTI-MRI scanning, 76

E

E-mail addiction, 56, 65

EEGs (electroencephalographs): identifying stored information using, 135; looking in the brain using, 73–74; measuring brain electrical activity using, 88

Ekman, P., 33, 133

Electrodes. *See* Implants/electrodes

Electroshock (electroconvulsive shock therapy), 49, 89, 93

Emotional brain (or limbic system), 4

Emotions: brain electrical activity linked to, 88; fear, 46, 53; "read" by fMRI, 133–134

Ephedrine (adrenaline), 25

Epigenetics: description of, 8; future research on directing, 19; memory research through study of, 52, 53–54; process of brain change through, 13–14

Epigenome (Web site), 14

Epilepsy, 20, 92, 109

Epinephrine (adrenaline), 46

Erasing bad memories, 48–50, 53

ESC-based therapy, 132

EST (electroshock therapy), 49, 89, 93

Eternal Sunshine of the Spotless Mind (film), 48, 49

Ethical Treatment of Human Embryos Act (Georgia), 132

Ethics. *See* Neuroethics

Exercise: boosting brain power through, 29, 35; memory enhancement through, 19

Extinction training, 53

F

Facebook, 56, 65, 69

Facial expression recognition, 133

Fantastic Voyage (film), 117

Fear: extinction training to overcome, 53; as memory maker, 46

FES (functional electrical stimulation), 93

Fields, R. D., 40, 77, 78–79

Fifth Amendment, 134

Fight-flight response, 52

Fisher, C., 89

"Flowers for Algernon" (short story), 26

fMRI (functional magnetic resonance imaging): can emotions be read by? 133–134; definition of, 74; Internet use brain activity measured by, 60; as lie detector, 133–134; limitations of, 79–80, 81; origins of, 83; process of taking, 74–76; recording brain activity while looking at images, 83; selection bias of, 80. *See also* MRI (magnetic resonance imaging)

Food and Drug Administration (FDA): ESC-based therapy clinical trials approved by, 132; side effects warnings on ADHD drugs by, 27; Vyvanse and Concerta approval by, 24

Forced psychopharmacological therapies, 137

Fourth Amendment, 134

Frontal lobotomy, 89, 90, 131

G

Gasser, U., 58

Gazzaniga, M. S., 48

Gene expression: brain function altered by, 8; memory formation and, 52; research on drug altering of, 14

Gene therapy: description of, 118–119, 123; the promise of, 123–125, 127–128

Genes: brief refresher course on, 124; epigenetics process of changing, 8, 13–14; long-term memory impact by, 52; NRXN3, 18; obesity and associated, 18. *See also* DNA (deoxyribonucleic acid)

Georgia's Ethical Treatment of Human Embryos Act, 132

Gibson, W., 62
Ginkgo balboa, 23
Glial cells, 78
God committees, 138
Google, 60, 65
Gould, E., 15
Gray, P., 66
Greely, H. T., 131, 135, 138
Greengard, P., 28
Gulf War PTSD, 48

H

Hallucinations, 28
Happiness contagion, 69
Harvard's Berkman Center for
    Internet and Society, 58
HATs (histone acetyltransferases),
    53
HDACs (histone daecetylases), 53,
    54
Hess, W. R., 88
Hindbrain (primitive brain or brain
    stem), 3–4
Hippocampus: animal studies on
    growth of neurons in, 15;
    description and function of, 4;
    DTI scanning to find anomalies
    in the, 76–77; new brain cells
    growth in, 10, 16; research on
    creating an artificial, 108–110
Hippocrates, 132
Histones, 53
Huntington's disease, 121, 125
Hurricane Katrina, 48

I

*iBrain: Surviving the Technological
    Alteration of the Modern Mind*
    (Small and Vorgan), 59
iBrain: bad, good, and unknown
    effects of, 59–61; balancing
    sensory self and, 64–65; of digital
    natives, 56–61
Identity, 51

Illes, G., 133
Illes, J., 133
Implants/electrodes: Alzheimer's
    disease treatment using, 96, 103;
    animal studies on radio-equipped
    electrodes, 89; cochlear, 106–107;
    current research on brain
    electricity and, 90–95; giving
    sight to the blind, 107–108;
    Orgasmatron for augmenting
    sexual function, 97; paralysis
    treatment using, 98, 102–103,
    110; possible future applications
    of, 103–104; radio-controlled
    amplified, 89, 93, 94–95, 104–
    106; research on downloading
    information using, 106–107.
    See also Bionic brain; Brain
    stimulation; Brain surgery
Infallible memory, 67
Information: brain research on
    downloading, 106–107; EEGs to
    identify stored, 135; Internet
    accessed, 59–61. *See also*
    Learning
Institute for the Future, 62
Institute of Psychiatry (King's
    College), 76
Internet: dating relationships using
    the, 113; digital natives' use of
    the, 56–57; digital social
    addiction to, 65; future brain
    implant for accessing, 62;
    information absorbed through
    the, 59–61; studies on brain
    activity and, 59–61
Involuntary sterilization, 131
IVIg (intravenous
    immunoglobulin), 43–44

J

Jichi Medical University (Japan),
    125
Johnny Mnemonic (film), 62

Jones, T. L., 50
Journal of Alzheimer's Disease, 44

K

Kabat-Zinn, J., 33
Kaiser Permanente, 33, 68, 115
Kansas State University, 111
Kennedy, P. R., 105, 110, 111
Kim, Y., 28
King's College (London), 76
Kringelbach, M. L., 91
Kurzweil, R., 62, 68, 116

L

Law, J., 112, 114
Learning: brain boosted through, 30; brain training programs and, 17–19; digital natives and interactive, 58–59; future research on neurons and, 20; neurogenesis connection to, 15–16; research on brain cells and effortful new, 16–17. *See also* Information
LeDoux, J., 39–40, 50, 51–52
Levy, D., 113
Li, J., 111
Lie to Me (TV series), 133
Limbic system (or emotional brain), 4
Liposomes, 126
Lobotomy, 89, 90, 131
"Love and Sex with Robots" (Levy), 114
Lying and brain scans, 133–134

M

MacArthur Foundation, 130
McCain, J., 56
McKoy, Leonard "Bones" (*Star Trek* character), 85
Macular degeneration, 108
Mad cow disease, 119
Mahesh, M., 32

Major depressive disorder, 50–51
Marijuana, 44–45
The Matrix (film), 103
Mayberg, H., 95, 99
Meditation: brain stimulation through, 31–35; description and methods of, 32; effect on amygdala by, 13; research on brain effects of, 33–35
MEG (magnetoencephalography), 74
Meloy, S., 97
Memex, 67
Memory Disorders Clinic (UCSD Medical Center), 42
Memory tricks, 47
Memory/memories: Alzheimer's disease and, 41–42; animal studies to restore, 54; chemistry of retaining, 45–47; consolidation of, 46; cybermemory research on, 63; digital brain to access, 67–69; erasing bad, 48–50, 53; exercise, diet, and social life enhancers of, 19; gene expression role in formation of, 52; identity connected to, 51; infallible, 67; mental illness, anxiety, and, 50–52; nature and qualities of, 38–39; predictions on neuroenhancers boosting, 2; storage and retrieval of, 39–40; then, now, and tomorrow research on, 5
Men in Black (film), 48, 50
Mental illness: anxiety and, 50–52; DBS (deep brain stimulation) treatment for, 90, 92, 94; electroshock treatment for, 49, 89, 93. *See also* Depression
Mental retardation, 2
Methodist Hospital (Houston), 84
Methylphenidate, 24, 28

Microglia (brain's immune cells), 122

Mind/Body Medical Institute, 33

Minority Report (film), 131, 134

Modafinil, 24

Mossman, K., 18

Movie boxes: *A.I.,* 112; *Brainstorm,* 63; *Eternal Sunshine of the Spotless Mind,* 49; "Flowers for Algernon" and *Charly,* 26; *Johnny Mnemonic,* 62; *Men in Black,* 50; *Minority Report,* 134; *Star Trek: The Next Generation,* 107; *The Terminal Man,* 91; *Total Recall,* 109. *See also* Brain fun facts; Science fiction

"Mozart effect," 30–31

MRI (magnetic resonance imaging): definition of, 74; as lie detector, 133–134; limitations of, 79–80; measuring changes in cerebral cortex, 27; measuring "memory centers," 42; origins and continuing development of, 83–85; process of taking, 74–76. *See also* fMRI (functional magnetic resonance imaging)

Multiple sclerosis, 103

Music stimulation, 30–31

Myelin (white matter), 77–79

MyLife Blob, 68

MyLifeBits, 68

MySpace, 56, 65

N

Nanomedicine, 125–127

Narcolepsy, 24

NASA, 115

National Eye Institute, 108

National Institute on Aging, 12

National Institute of Child Health and Human Development, 40

National Institute of Mental Health, 27

National Institutes of Health (NIH), 1, 14, 33, 41, 77, 115

National Nanotechnology Initiative (2010), 127

National Science Foundation, 109

Nazi scientific experiments, 131

Neural shifting speed, 58

Neural Signals, Inc., 105, 110

Neurally augmented sexual function, 97

Neuroenhancers: military applications of, 3; predictions on future use of, 2

Neuroenhancing drugs, 22–24

Neuroethics: ADHD drugs and issue of, 137–138; brain scans as lie detectors, 133–134; brain scans and privacy, bias, and self-incrimination, 136–137; forced psychopharmacological therapies, 137; future issues related to, 138–140; legal applications of brain scans, 134–136; origins and issues of, 130–132; stem cells controversy, 132–133. *See also* Brain research

Neurogenesis: description of, 8, 10; learning connection to, 15–16; new brain cells produced through, 10–11; research on prompting, 19–20

Neuroimaging. *See* Brain scans (neuroimaging)

Neuromorphing, 106–107

Neuron Glia Biology (journal), 77

Neuronal ceroid ipofuscinosis (Batten disease), 121

Neurons: Alzheimer's disease research on, 42; animal studies on growth in hippocampus, 15,

16; fight-flight response controlled by, 52; future research on learning and, 20; PKMzeta studies on strengthening memory networks of, 50; research on changing population codes of, 107; research on interfacing abiotic machines with, 108; research on thought-driven devices and, 110–112; studies on growth of, 10–11; synapses between, 39, 51, 78, 112, 114

Neuroplasticity: description of, 8, 11; examples of brain network repairs through, 11–13; research on how to encourage, 19

Neurosurgery. *See* Brain surgery

Neurotechnology Industry Report (2008), 3

Neurotransmitters: acetylcholine, 24, 44; antidepressant blockage of, 25; as communication networks, 3; dopamine, 25, 28

New York Neural Stem Cell Institute, 122

New York Times, 48

New York University, 39

Nicotine, 46

9/11, 48

No Lie MRI Company, 135

Nootrope, 23

NRXN3 gene, 18

NSAIDs (nonsteroidal anti-inflammatory drugs), 43

Nucleus accumbens, 25

Nuvigil, 23

O

Obama, B., 56, 132

Obesity, 18

Object play, 67

Office of Science (DOE), 108

Omega-3s, 23, 29, 43

One Flew over the Cuckoo's Nest (film), 89

Open monitoring meditation, 32

Orbitofrontal cortex, 76

Orgasmatron, 97

The Other Brain (Fields), 77

P

Pain: brain signature for, 99; implanting spinal electrodes to alleviate, 97

Palfrey, J., 58

Paralysis: implant treatment of, 98, 102–103, 110; stem cells and spinal cord injury repair, 121

Parkinson's disease: future of electrodes treatment of, 92, 98, 109; gene therapy studies on, 125; past, current, and future research on, 2, 5; promise of gene therapy for, 124; research on stimulating neurons to allay, 111

Peckham, H., 111

Pedophiles, 76

People's name memory, 47

Periodic Table of Elements, 40

PET (positron emission tomography), 74

Phrenology (pseudoscience), 72

Pittsburgh Healthy Women Study, 18

PKMzeta studies, 50

"Plato's cave" technique, 84

Pleasure center (or reward circuit), 4

Population codes, 107

Prefrontal cortex, 25, 77, 82

Prensky, M., 56–57

Primitive brain (brain stem or hindbrain), 3–4

Project on Law and Neuroscience, 130

Prosthetics research, 2, 110
Proteasomes, 47
Provigil, 23, 24
Psychopathy diagnosis/treatment, 76
PTSD (post-traumatic stress disorder), 48, 51
"Puzzlingly High Correlations in fMRI Studies of Emotion, Personality and Social Cognition" (Vul and associates), 80

R
Radio-controlled amplified electrodes: animal studies on, 89; bionic brain research on, 104–106; medical treatments using, 93; new technology improving use of, 94–95
Rainbows End (Vinge), 41–42, 61–62
The Relaxation Response (Benson), 33
Research Center for Information Law (University of St. Gallen), 58
Retinitis pigmentosa, 108
Rhesus monkeys studies, 28
Ritalin: ADHA treated with, 23, 24; dosage issue of, 25–26
RNA (ribonucleic acid), 52, 119, 124
Roadmap Epigenomics Program, 14
"Robot love" science fiction, 112, 113
Rockefeller University, 28
Rodent University, 15
Röntgen radiation (X-ray), 73
Rötgen, W. C., 73
RPE (retinal pigment epithelium), 122–123

S
Safire, W., 132
St. John's wort, 23

School of Public Health (University of California, Berkeley), 24
Science fiction: on brain-machine interface, cyborgs, "robot love," 104, 113; *Fantastic Voyage* brain surgery, 118; on memory implants, 109; *Minority Report* neuroethics of, 131; on "smart pills," 26. *See also* Movie boxes
Scientific American, 40, 81, 109, 131, 139
Scientific American Mind, 18, 80
Second Sight, 108
"See Spot run" neural code, 107, 109
Semel Institute for Neuroscience and human Behavior (UCLA), 59
Sensory integration therapy, 66–67
Sensory self: balancing the iBrain and, 64–65; digital natives and heightened visual, 58
Serotonin, 25
Sex robots, 112, 113
Sexual orientation, 90
Shaw, P., 27
Shermer, M., 80, 81
Shorthand communication, 58
The Six Million Dollar Man (TV series), 104, 108, 115
Skeptic Magazine, 80
Sleeper (film), 97
Small, G., 59, 60
"Smart drugs": *Charly* (film) on, 26; research on dosage issue of, 25–26; safety issues related to, 26–28; types of, 24–25
Smith, W., 50
Snyder, P., 18
Social interaction: childhood play for developing normal, 66–67; digital social addiction, 65; happiness as contagious through physical, 69

Social play, 67
SPECT (single photon emission computed tomography), 74
Stanford University, 131, 132
Stanford University study (2002), 59
Star Trek (TV series), 85
Star Trek: The Next Generation (TV series), 107
Stem cell therapy: animal studies on stroke, 122; neuroethical controversy over, 132–133; the promise of, 118–119, 127–128
Stem cells: overview of, 120–121; research on, 121; RPE (retinal pigment epithelium), 122–123
Stix, G., 109
Stors, T., 15
Striatum, 77
Strokes: hippocampus damage during, 109; neural prostheses for, 103
SUNY Downstate, 50
Swaminathan, N., 83
Synapses: challenges of studying, 78; description of, 39; measuring activity of, 114; memory held in connections of, 39; protein synthesis to strengthen, 51

T
Tabula rasa, 6
Tactile sensations, 64–65
tDCS (transcranial direct current stimulation), 93–94
Technology: bad, good, and unknown effects of, 59–61; bionic brain hurdles related to, 114–116; cell phone, 61; continuing interest and research on digital, 63; developing electrical brain stimulation, 97–100; digital natives' adoption of, 56–57; digital social addiction to, 65; interactive learning through, 58–59; nanotechnology, 125–127; new 3-D video, 84; speculations on future of digital, 67–69. *See also* Brain scans (neuroimaging)
Temple, S., 122
Temporal codes, 107
The Terminal Man (film), 91
Thalamus, 4
THC (tetrahydrocannabinol), 45
Thinking brain, 4
Thought-driven devices, 110–112
3-D video technology, 84
TMS (transcranial magnetic stimulation), 92–93
Total Recall (film), 109
Tourette's syndrome, 90, 92
Transcendental meditation (TM), 32
Trauma: erasing memories of, 49; PTSD (posttraumatic stress disorder), 48, 51
Turmeric (curcumin), 43
Tuskegee syphilis study (1942), 131
Twitter, 65

U
Uncinate fasciculus, 76
University of Bonn (Germany), 76
University of British Columbia, 133
University of California, Berkeley, 24, 83
University of California, San Francisco, 33
University of Maastricht (Netherlands), 114
University of Oxford (UK), 91
University of Pennsylvania, 125
University of St. Gallen (Switzerland), 58
University of South Carolina, 109
University of Toronto (Canada), 50
University of Wisconsin, 34

U.S. Defense Advanced Research
   Projects Agency (DARPA):
   artificial hippocampus research
   by, 109; brain-machine interface
   research investment by, 115;
   computer-mediated telepathy
   research by, 86; cybermemory
   research by, 63; downloading
   information research by, 107;
   sponsoring research in
   prosthetics for veterans, 110
U.S. Department of Energy's Office
   of Science, 108
U.S. Food and Drug Administration
   (FDA), 24, 27, 132

V
Video games stimulation, 30
Vinge, V., 61
Visual cortex, 9
Visual senses: digital natives and
   heightened, 58; implants giving
   vision to the blind, 108
Vitamin E, 43
"Voodoo Correlations in Social
   Neuroscience" (Vul and
   associates), 80
Vorgan, G., 59

Vul, E., 80
Vyvanse, 24

W
Wake Forest University Baptist
   Medical Center, 44, 47
Walter, J., 14
Welch, R., 118
White matter (myelin): description
   and function of, 78; description
   of, 77; DTI imaging of, 78–79;
   pedophiles and anomalies in,
   76
WiFi connection, 56, 57
Winslet, K., 49
Woodruff, B., 11–12
World Stem Cell Summit (2009),
   122

X
X-ray, 73

Y
Yale University School of Medicine,
   28

Z
Zen meditation, 32